Annie's

Lap & Throw Quilts

LEISURE ARTS, INC. • Maumelle, Arkansas

Sometimes it's nice to have an entire book dedicated to a certain size quilt. Not everyone wants to make large quilts. Sometimes a lap or throw size is just what you're looking for. Here's a single book of smaller quilts perfect to use for gifts, charity, baby or throws. With a bit of imagination and your fabric selection, you will have endless possibilities for lovely quilts. You will use this collection of 12 wonderful patterns again and again for all your quilting needs. *Lap & Throw Quilts* has something for everyone. It has all skill levels and quilt styles ranging from traditional to modern. It is destined to be a favorite go-to book with its timeless designs.

ENJOY!

ANNIE'S STAFF

EDITOR **Carolyn S. Vagts**
CREATIVE DIRECTOR **Brad Snow**
PUBLISHING SERVICES DIRECTOR **Brenda Gallmeyer**
MANAGING EDITOR **Barb Sprunger**
TECHNICAL EDITOR **Angie Buckles**
COPY MANAGER **Corene Painter**
SENIOR COPY EDITOR **Emily Carter**
TECHNICAL ARTIST **Amanda Joseph**
SENIOR PRODUCTION ARTIST **Nicole Gage**
PRODUCTION ARTISTS **Glenda Chamberlain, Edith Teegarden**
PRODUCTION ASSISTANTS **Laurie Lehman, Marj Morgan, Judy Neuenschwander**
PHOTOGRAPHY SUPERVISOR **Tammy Christian**
PHOTOGRAPHY **Matthew Owen**
PHOTO STYLISTS **Tammy Liechty, Tammy Steiner**

CHIEF EXECUTIVE OFFICER **David McKee**
EXECUTIVE VICE PRESIDENT **Michele Fortune**

LEISURE ARTS STAFF
Editorial Staff
CREATIVE ART DIRECTOR **Katherine Laughlin**
PUBLICATIONS DIRECTOR **Leah Lampirez**
SPECIAL PROJECTS DIRECTOR **Susan Frantz Wiles**
PREPRESS TECHNICIAN **Stephanie Johnson**

Business Staff
PRESIDENT AND CHIEF EXECUTIVE OFFICER **Fred F. Pruss**
SENIOR VICE PRESIDENT OF OPERATIONS **Jim Dittrich**
VICE PRESIDENT OF RETAIL SALES **Martha Adams**
CHIEF FINANCIAL OFFICER **Tiffany P. Childers**
CONTROLLER **Teresa Eby**
INFORMATION TECHNOLOGY DIRECTOR **Brian Roden**
DIRECTOR OF E-COMMERCE **Mark Hawkins**
MANAGER OF E-COMMERCE **Robert Young**

Library of Congress Control Number: 2014955820
ISBN-13/EAN: 978-1-4647-3336-9
UPC: 0-28906-06443-8

PROJECTS

Spring Baskets

Whether you're picking flowers or gathering berries, these jaunty baskets hold the feeling of the season.

Designed & Quilted by Tricia Lynn Maloney

Skill Level
Confident Beginner

Finished Size
Quilt Size: 55" x 55"
Block Size: 9" x 9" finished
Number of Blocks: 16

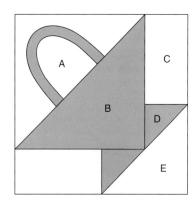

Basket
9" x 9" Finished Block
Make 16

CUTTING

From red print:
- Cut 1 (7⅝" x 21") strip.
  Subcut 2 (7⅝") squares. Cut each square in half on 1 diagonal to make 4 B triangles.
- Cut 1 (3⅛" x 21") strip.
  Subcut 4 (3⅛") squares. Cut each square In half on 1 diagonal to make 8 D triangles.
- Cut 1 (5" x 21") strip.
  Subcut 4 (5") squares for handles.

From aqua print:
- Cut 1 (7⅝" x 21") strip.
  Subcut 1 (7⅝") square. Cut square in half on 1 diagonal to make 2 B triangles.
- Cut 2 (3⅛") squares.
  Subcut each square in half on 1 diagonal to make 4 D triangles.
- Cut 1 (5" x 21") strip.
  Subcut 2 (5") squares for handles.

From aqua dot:
- Cut 2 (2½" x 42") strips.
  Subcut 25 (2½") G squares.

From aqua squares:

- Cut 1 (7⅝" x 42") strip.
  Subcut 3 (7⅝") squares. Cut each square in half on 1 diagonal to make 6 B triangles.
- Cut 6 (3⅛") squares.
  Subcut each square in half on 1 diagonal to make 12 D triangles.
- Cut 1 (5" x 42") strip.
  Subcut 6 (5") squares for handles.

From white solid:

- Cut 2 (7⅝" x 42") strips.
  Subcut 8 (7⅝") squares. Cut each square in half on 1 diagonal to make 16 A triangles.
- Cut 4 (2¾" x 42") strips.
  Subcut 32 (2¾" x 5") C rectangles.
- Cut 2 (5⅜" x 42") strips.
  Subcut 8 (5⅜") squares. Cut each square in half on 1 diagonal to make 16 E triangles.

From red/aqua print:

- Cut 1 (7⅝" x 42") strip.
  Subcut 2 (7⅝") squares. Cut each square in half on 1 diagonal to make 4 B triangles.
- Cut 4 (3⅛") squares.
  Subcut each square in half on 1 diagonal to make 8 D triangles.
- Cut 1 (5" x 42") strip.
  Subcut 4 (5") squares for handles.
- Cut 5 (5" x 42") H/I strips.

From red check:

- Cut 3 (9½" x 42") strips.
  Subcut 40 (2½" x 9½") F strips.
- Cut 6 (2¼" x 42") binding strips.

PREPARING THE HANDLES

1. Trace the handle shape given on next page onto the paper side of the fusible web leaving ½" between pieces; cut out shapes, leaving a margin around each one.
2. Fuse the paper shapes to the wrong side of the previously cut 5" squares; cut out handle shapes on the traced lines. Remove paper backing.

COMPLETING THE BASKET BLOCKS

1. To complete one Basket block, select one each A and E triangle and two C rectangles. Select the following from one print: one handle, one B triangle and two D triangles.
2. Sew D to the end of C to make a C-D unit as shown in Figure 1; press seam toward D. Repeat to make a reverse C-D unit, again referring to Figure 1.

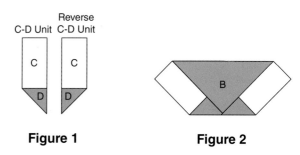

Figure 1   **Figure 2**

3. Sew the C-D and reverse C-D units to opposite sides of B to make a B-C-D unit as shown in Figure 2; press seams away from B.
4. Center and fuse the handle shape to A referring to Figure 3. Using contrasting thread and a narrow zigzag stitch, sew around edges of handle to secure handle to A.

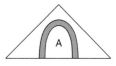

Figure 3

5. Sew the A/handle unit and E to the B-C-D unit to complete one Basket block referring to Figure 4; press seams toward B and E.

Figure 4

6. Repeat steps 1–5 to complete a total of two aqua print, six aqua squares print and four each red print and red/aqua print Basket blocks.

COMPLETING THE QUILT

1. Select one block each aqua print, aqua squares print, red print, and red/aqua print and five F strips. Join the blocks with the F strips to make Row 1 as shown in Figure 5; press seams toward F strips. Repeat to make a second row for Row 4.

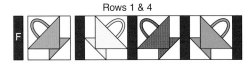

Rows 1 & 4

Figure 5

2. Select one block each red print and red/aqua print and two aqua squares print blocks and five F strips. Join the blocks with F strips to make Row 2 as shown in Figure 6; press seams toward F. Repeat to make a second row for Row 3.

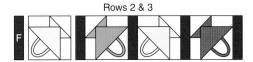

Rows 2 & 3

Figure 6

3. Select and join four F strips and five G squares to make a sashing row referring to Figure 7; press seams toward F strips. Repeat to make a total of five sashing rows.

Sashing Row
Make 5

Figure 7

4. Arrange and join the block rows with the sashing rows referring to the Assembly Diagram for positioning of rows; press seams toward the sashing rows.

5. Join H/I strips on short ends to make a long strip; press seams open. Subcut strip into two each 5" x 46½" H strips and 5" x 55½" I strips.

6. Sew H strips to the top and bottom and I strips to opposite sides of the pieced center to complete the quilt top; press seams toward H and I strips.

7. Create a quilt sandwich referring to Quilting Basics on page 62.

8. Quilt as desired.

9. Bind referring to Quilting Basics on page 62 to finish. ●

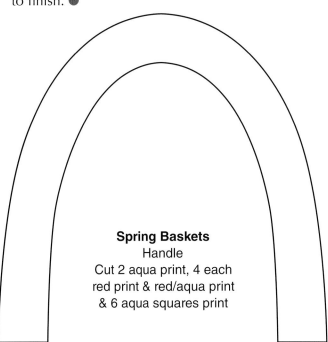

Spring Baskets
Handle
Cut 2 aqua print, 4 each
red print & red/aqua print
& 6 aqua squares print

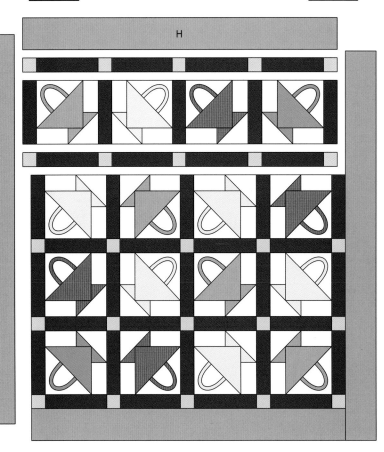

Spring Baskets
Assembly Diagram 55" x 55"

Triangle Fever

This quilt is the perfect project for showcasing your scrap collection.

Designed & Quilted by Maria Umhey

Skill Level
Intermediate

Finished Size
Quilt Size: 49" x 57"
Block Size: 6⅞" x 8" finished
Number of Blocks: 63

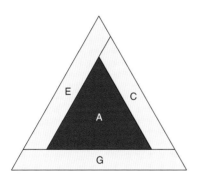

Dark Triangle
6⅞" x 8" Finished Block
Make 31

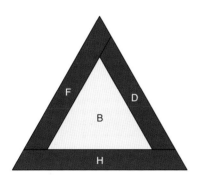

Light Triangle
6⅞" x 8" Finished Block
Make 32

CUTTING
Refer to Template Cutting instructions to cut light and dark print scraps.

From navy print:
- Cut 5 (4" x 42") Q/R strips.

From gold tonal:
- Cut 5 (1½" x 42") O/P strips.
- Cut 6 (2½" x 42") binding strips.

TEMPLATE CUTTING

1. Prepare templates using patterns given; cut A/B and I/J pieces as directed on patterns.
2. Referring to Figure 1 and using the remaining templates, cut one each C, E and G set from each 1½"-wide light strip and one each D, F and H set from each 1½"-wide dark strip. Repeat to cut a set of K and M pieces from the remainder of four light strips; a set of KR and MR pieces from the remainder of four light strips; a set of L and N pieces from the remainder of three dark strips; and a set of LR and NR pieces from the remainder of three dark strips. *Note: This quilt would be a great place to use a 60-degree quilter's ruler, instead of project templates.*

Figure 1

COMPLETING THE TRIANGLE BLOCKS

1. To complete one Dark Triangle block, select one set of matching C, E and G pieces.
2. Sew C to the right side edge and E to the left side edge of A as shown in Figure 2; press seams toward C and then E.

Figure 2

3. Add a G strip along the bottom edge of A to complete one Dark Triangle block; press seam toward G.
4. Repeat steps 1–3 to complete 31 Dark Triangle blocks.
5. Repeat steps 1–3 with B, D, F and H pieces to complete 32 Light Triangle blocks referring to the block drawing.

COMPLETING THE EDGE UNITS

1. Sew K to the left side edge of I and add M to the bottom short edge to complete one dark side unit as shown in Figure 3; press seams toward K and then M. Repeat with KR, MR and IR pieces to make a reversed dark side unit, again referring to Figure 3. Repeat to make four each dark side units and reversed dark side units.

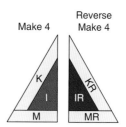

Figure 3

2. Repeat step 4 with J/JR, L/LR and N/NR pieces to complete three each light side units and reversed light side units as shown in Figure 4.

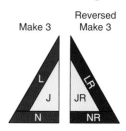

Figure 4

COMPLETING THE QUILT

1. Select five Light Triangle blocks and four Dark Triangle blocks and one each dark side and reversed dark side units. Join to make an X row as shown in Figure 5; press seams toward Light Triangle blocks. Repeat to make four X rows.

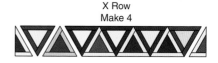

Figure 5

2. Select five Dark Triangle blocks and four Light Triangle blocks, and one each light side and reversed light side units. Join to make a Y row as shown in Figure 6; press seams toward Light Triangle blocks. Repeat to make three Y rows.

Y Row
Make 3

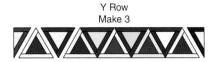

Figure 6

3. Arrange and join the X and Y rows to complete the pieced top referring to the Assembly Diagram for positioning of rows; press seams in one direction.
4. Join the O/P strips on short ends to make one long strip; press seams open. Subcut strip into two 40½" O strips and two 50½" P strips.
5. Sew O strips to the top and bottom and P strips to opposite long sides; press seams toward O and P strips.
6. Join the Q/R strips on short ends to make one long strip; press seam open. Subcut strip into two 42½" Q strips and two 57½" R strips.
7. Sew Q strips to the top and bottom and R strips to opposite long sides of the pieced center; press seams toward Q and R strips to complete the pieced top.
8. Layer and quilt referring to Quilting Basics on page 62, except trim batting and backing 1" larger all around.
9. Join the binding strips on short ends to make one long strip; press seams open.
10. Press under ¼" along one long side.
11. Pin and stitch the raw edge of the right side of the binding even with the raw edge of the right side of the pieced top with batting/backing extending as shown in Figure 7, mitering corners and overlapping at the beginning and end.

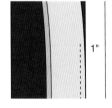

1"

Figure 7

12. Press the binding strip to the right side and over the extending backing and batting; turn excess to the wrong side of the quilt and hand-stitch in place to finish. *Note: The binding looks like a narrow border all around the outside of the quilt.* ●

Triangle Fever
Assembly Diagram 49" x 57"

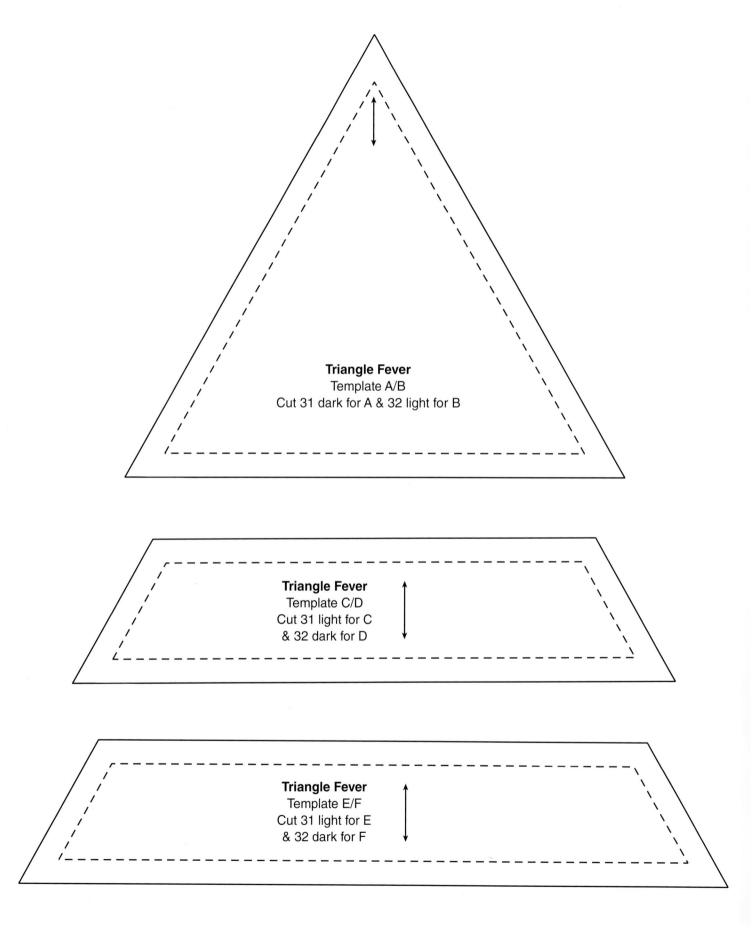

Triangle Fever
Template A/B
Cut 31 dark for A & 32 light for B

Triangle Fever
Template C/D
Cut 31 light for C
& 32 dark for D

Triangle Fever
Template E/F
Cut 31 light for E
& 32 dark for F

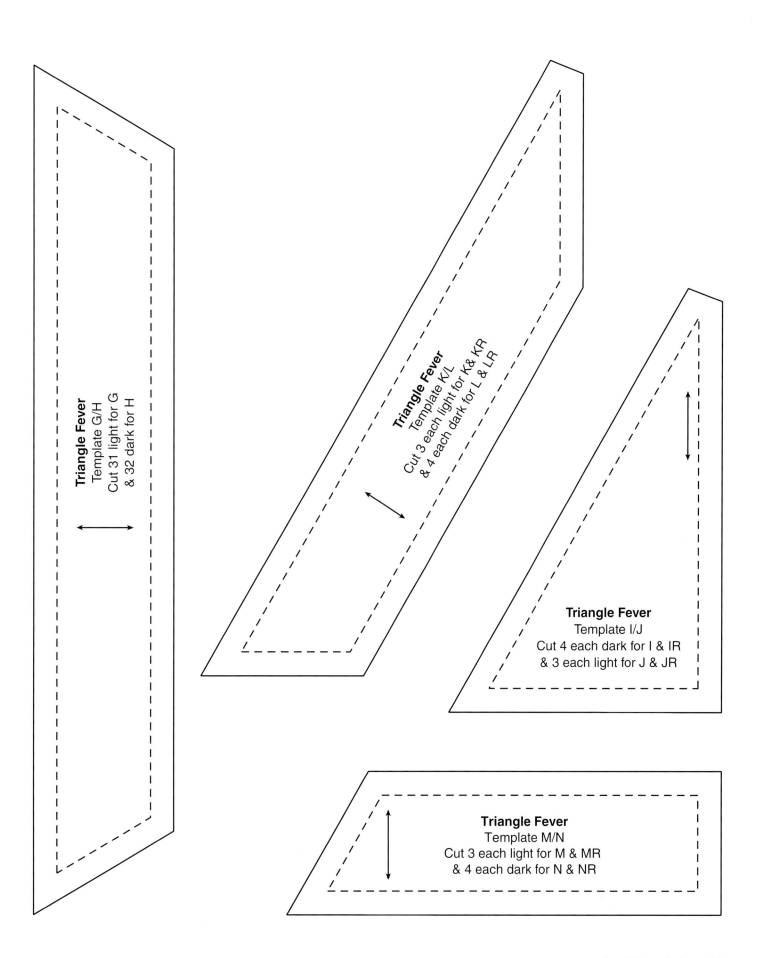

Triangle Fever
Template G/H
Cut 31 light for G
& 32 dark for H

Triangle Fever
Template K/L
Cut 3 each light for K& KR
& 4 each dark for L & LR

Triangle Fever
Template I/J
Cut 4 each dark for I & IR
& 3 each light for J & JR

Triangle Fever
Template M/N
Cut 3 each light for M & MR
& 4 each dark for N & NR

Modern Comfort

Use precut 10" squares cut twice on the diagonal to quickly stitch together this contemporary quilt. When choosing squares, select half light fabrics and half dark fabrics.

Design by Connie Kauffman

Skill Level
Beginner

Finished Size
Quilt Size: 52½" x 65½"

MATERIALS

- 13 coordinating light precut 10" squares
- 21 coordinating dark precut 10" squares
- ½ yard rust tonal
- ⅞ yard green floral
- 1 yard black tonal
- Batting to size
- Backing to size
- Thread
- Template material
- 2 (9" x 12") sheets fusible web
- Basic sewing tools and supplies

CUTTING

From light precut squares:
- Cut 13 light 10" squares in half on both diagonals to make 52 light A triangles.
  Select 50 light triangles for piecing.

From dark precut squares:
- Cut 19 dark 10" squares in half on both diagonals to make 76 dark A triangles.
  Select 57 dark triangles for piecing; set aside remaining dark triangles for fused triangles.
  Trim the two remaining dark 10" squares to make two 5¼" squares; cut the squares in half on one diagonal to make a total of four B triangles. Set aside one B triangle of each color for another project.
- Prepare a template for J using pattern given; trace the J template onto the paper side of the fusible web 16 times as shown in Figure 1. Cut out triangles leaving a small margin around each one; fuse the triangles to the wrong side of the leftover dark A triangles. Cut out the J triangles on the marked lines; remove paper backing.

Trace 8 J triangles on each sheet

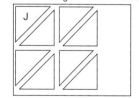

Figure 1

From rust tonal:
- Cut 5 (2½" by fabric width) strips rust tonal.
  Join strips on short ends to make one long strip; press seams open. Subcut strip into 2 (2½" x 53") C strips and 2 (2½" x 44") D strips.

From green floral:

- Cut 6 (4" by fabric width) strips.
  Join strips on short ends to make one long strip; press seams open. Subcut into 2 (4" x 59") G strips and 2 (4" x 53") H strips.

From black tonal:

- Cut 5 (1½" by fabric width) strips.
  Join strips on short ends to make one long strip; press seams open. Subcut into 2 (1½" x 57") E strips and 2 (1½" x 46") F strips.
- Cut 6 (2¼" by fabric width) binding.
- Cut 1 (7½" by fabric width) strip.
  Subcut strip into 4 (7½") I squares.

COMPLETING THE QUILT

1. Join a light and dark A triangle to make an A-A unit as shown in Figure 2; press seam to one side. Repeat to make 44 A-A units.

Make 44

Figure 2

2. Arrange and join the A-A units in diagonal rows with the remaining A triangles at ends of the rows and B triangles at two corners referring to Figure 3; press seams in adjoining rows in opposite directions.

Figure 3

3. Join the rows to complete the pieced center; press seams in one direction.

4. Randomly center and fuse a J triangle on the light side of 16 A-A units referring to the Assembly Diagram.

5. Using a decorative machine stitch and a variety of thread colors, stitch around the edges of each J triangle.

6. Sew C strips to opposite long sides and D strips to the top and bottom of the pieced center; press seams toward C and D strips.

7. Repeat step 6 with the E and F strips and then the G and H strips, referring to the Assembly Diagram for positioning; press seams toward strips as you sew.

8. Draw a diagonal line from corner to corner on the wrong side of each I square.

9. Place an I square on one corner of the G/H borders and stitch on the marked line as shown in Figure 4. Trim seam to ¼" and press I to the right side, again referring to Figure 4.

Figure 4

10. Repeat step 9, stitching an I square to each corner to complete the pieced top.

11. Create a quilt sandwich referring to Quilting Basics on page 62.

12. Quilt as desired.

13. Bind referring to Quilting Basics on page 62 to finish. ●

Modern Comfort
Template J
Cut as per instructions

Modern Comfort
Assembly Diagram 52½" x 65½"

Pretty in Pink

Piece this quick and easy quilt with one block and two fabrics in a day.

Designed & Quilted by Julie Weaver

Skill Level
Beginner

Finished Size
Quilt Size: 50" x 62"
Block Size: 6" x 6" finished
Number of Blocks: 48

MATERIALS

- ¾ yard cream solid
- 1⅜ yards cream-with-pink dots
- 2⅝ yards pink-with-cream dots
- Backing to size
- Batting to size
- Thread
- Basic sewing tools and supplies

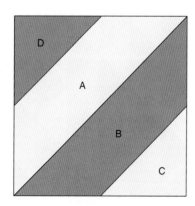

Pretty in Pink
6" x 6" Finished Block
Make 48

CUTTING

From cream solid:
- Cut 10 (2" by fabric width) E/F/I/J strips.

From cream-with-pink dots:
- Cut 4 (6⅞" by fabric width) strips.
  Subcut strips into 24 (6⅞") A squares.
- Cut 4 (3½" by fabric width) strips.
  Subcut strips into 48 (3½") C squares.

From pink-with-cream dots:
- Cut 4 (6⅞" by fabric width) strips.
  Subcut strips into 24 (6⅞") B squares.
- Cut 4 (3½" by fabric width) strips.
  Subcut strips into 48 (3½") D squares.
- Cut 5 (4½" by fabric width) G/H strips.
- Cut 6 (2¼" by fabric width) binding strips.

COMPLETING THE BLOCKS

1. Draw a diagonal line from corner to corner on the wrong side of each A, C and D square.
2. Referring to Figure 1, place an A square right sides together with a B square and stitch ¼" on each side of the marked line. Cut apart on the marked line; open and press units with seams toward B to complete two A-B units.

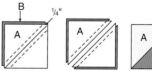

Figure 1

3. Referring to Figure 2, place a C square right sides together on the B corner of each A-B unit and stitch on the marked line. Trim seam to ¼" and press C to the right side.

Figure 2

4. Referring to Figure 3, repeat step 3 with a marked D square on the A corner of the A-B-C units; trim seams to ¼" and press D to the right side to complete two Pretty in Pink blocks.

Figure 3

5. Repeat steps 2–4 to complete a total of 48 Pretty in Pink blocks.

COMPLETING THE QUILT

1. Arrange and join six Pretty in Pink blocks to make a horizontal row 1 referring to Figure 4; press seams in one direction. Repeat to make a total of four row 1's.

Row 1
Make 4

Figure 4

2. Repeat step 1 to make a total of four horizontal row 2's referring to Figure 5.

Row 2
Make 4

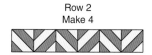

Figure 5

3. Join the rows alternating rows 1 and 2 to complete the quilt center referring to the Assembly Diagram; press seams in one direction.

4. Join the E/F/I/J strips on the short ends to make a long strip; press. Subcut strip into two strips each as follows: 2" x 48½" E, 2" x 39½" F, 2" x 59½" I and 2" x 50½" J.

5. Sew E strips to opposite long sides and F strips to the top and bottom of the quilt center referring to the Assembly Diagram; press seams toward the E and F strips.

6. Repeat step 4 with G/H strips to cut two 4½" x 51½" G strips and two 4½" x 47½" H strips.

7. Sew G strips to opposite sides and H strips to the top and bottom of the pieced center; press seams toward G and H strips.

8. Sew I strips on opposite sides and J strips on the top and bottom of the quilt center to complete the quilt top. Press seams toward the I and J strips.

9. Create a quilt sandwich referring to Quilting Basics on page 62.

10. Quilt as desired.

11. Bind referring to Quilting Basics on page 62 to finish. ●

Pressing Tip

It's important to pay close attention to pressing when making this project. There are lots of seams, and in order for everything to fit properly, one must press, press, press! Press the blocks in each row in the opposite direction of the next row so that the blocks will lock together when joining the rows.

To get the seams of the blocks to lock when sewing the rows, if necessary, pin one of the seams in the opposite direction from the original direction it was pressed. Then clip into the seam on the back side to allow the rest of the seam to go back to its original pressing direction (Figure A). Sometimes it is just not possible to press all seams in the proper direction for joining later.

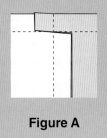

Figure A

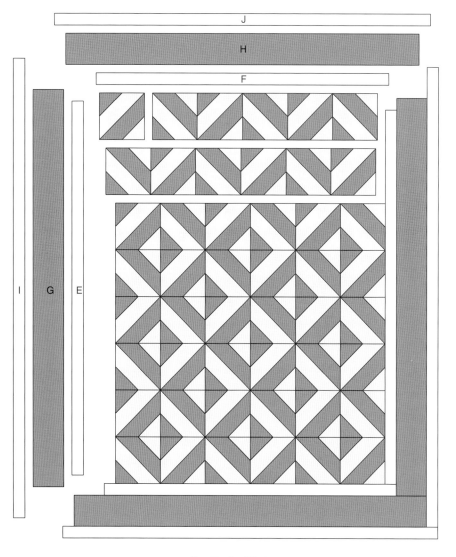

Pretty in Pink
Assembly Diagram 50" x 62"

Red Delicious

It's apple harvest time! Our red delicious quilt is fresh-picked just for you.

Designed & Quilted by Darlene Leosh

Skill Level
Intermediate

Finished Size
Quilt Size: 68" x 68"
Block Size: 8" x 8" finished
Number of Blocks: 64

MATERIALS

- ⅝ yard each 5 reproduction prints
- 1⅛ yards red tonal
- 1⅛ yards white tonal
- 3¾ yards yellow tonal
- Backing to size
- Batting to size
- Thread
- Fabric glue
- Basic sewing tools and supplies

CUTTING

From reproduction prints:
- Cut 4 (3" x 42") strips from each print.
  Subcut 50 (3") C squares for a total of 250.
- Cut a total of 7 (1¼" x 42") strips.
  Subcut 14 (1¼" x 21") F strips.
- Cut a total of 7 (2¼" x 42") binding strips.

From red tonal:
- Cut 7 (4¾" x 42") strips.
  Subcut 50 (4¾") B squares. Set aside for Special Cutting instructions.

From white tonal:
- Cut 7 (4¾" x 42") strips.
  Subcut 50 (4¾") E squares.

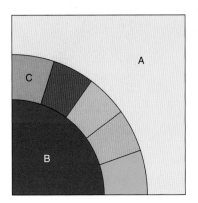

Red Delicious
8" x 8" Finished Block
Make 14

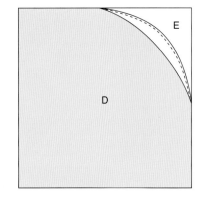

Folded Square
8" x 8" Finished Block
Make 14

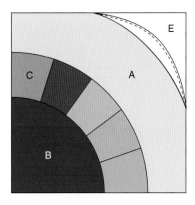

Folded Red Delicious
8" x 8" Finished Block
Make 36

From yellow tonal:

- Cut 4 (8½" x 42") strips.
  Subcut 14 (8½") D squares.
- Cut 9 (8½" x 42") strips. Set aside for Special Cutting instructions.
- Cut 7 (2½" x 42") G/H strips.

SPECIAL CUTTING

1. Prepare templates for A and B using patterns given.
2. Place the B template on the red tonal B squares and trim to size.
3. Place the A template on the 8½" x 42" yellow tonal strips and cut pieces as directed and referring to Figure 1.

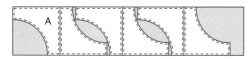

Figure 1

COMPLETING THE PAPER-PIECED UNITS

1. Make 50 copies of the arc paper-piecing pattern on page 27 onto foundation paper.
2. Reduce your machine's stitch length to 1.8 or 1.5.
3. Select one C square of each of the five prints and arrange the fabrics in the order they will appear in the arc. When satisfied with placement, number pieces from 1–5. Stack all same-fabric pieces in the same number order for use in future piecing to keep the same color order on all arcs.
4. Place the fabric 3 square right side up on the unmarked side of the foundation paper, center it over area 3 on the foundation paper. Hold in place with a pin or a dab of fabric glue stick. *Note: The fabric should extend past the edges of area 3 approximately ¼" on all sides for a good seam allowance.*
5. Turn the foundation paper over to the marked side and fold on the line between areas 3 and 4, exposing fabric 3 as shown in Figure 2.
6. Trim the exposed fabric to approximately ¼" from the folded paper edge; lay foundation paper flat and repeat process between areas 2 and 3.

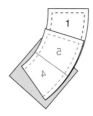

Figure 2

7. Lay foundation paper flat and turn over with unmarked side up; align fabric 4 right side down on fabric 3, matching the fabric edges between areas 3 and 4 as shown in Figure 3. Make any adjustments in fabric 4's placement to ensure that it will completely cover area 4 after sewing.

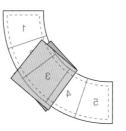

Figure 3   **Figure 4**

8. Holding both fabrics in place, turn the foundation over to the marked side and sew on the line separating areas 3 and 4, stitching to the outside edge of the pattern as shown in Figure 4.
9. Trim the seam allowance of the two stitched pieces to ¼" or less. Flip piece 4 to the right side and finger-press in place as shown in Figure 5.
10. Hold foundation up to the light with fabric side away from you. The edges of fabric 4 should extend past the area 4 lines by ¼". If placement is correct, press in place with a dry iron.

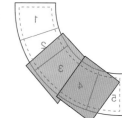

Figure 5

11. Turn foundation paper over to the marked side and fold the foundation paper on the line between areas 4 and 5 exposing fabric 4. Trim the exposed fabric to ¼" from the folded paper edge.
12. Lay the foundation paper flat and turn over with un-marked side up. Align fabric 5 right sides together on fabric 4, matching the fabric edges between areas 4 and 5. Make any adjustments in fabric 5's placement to ensure that it will completely cover area 5 after sewing. Repeat steps 8–11.
13. Add fabrics 2 and 1 in the same way until the foundation is covered.
14. Press and trim through all layers on the outermost lines of the foundation paper.
15. Repeat steps 4–14 to complete 49 more pieced arcs; do not remove paper at this time.

COMPLETING THE RED DELICIOUS BLOCKS

1. Fold each A and B piece to find the center of the curved edge and crease to mark.

2. To complete one Red Delicious block, pin B right sides together with one pieced arc, matching centers as shown in Figure 6; stitch along the printed line on the foundation paper. Clip edges on the B piece; press seams toward B.

Figure 6

3. Repeat step 2 with A on the opposite side of the pieced arc to complete one Red Delicious block; press seam toward A.

4. Repeat steps 2 and 3 to complete 50 Red Delicious blocks.

5. Remove paper from pieced arcs.

COMPLETING THE FOLDED RED DELICIOUS BLOCKS

1. Select 36 Red Delicious blocks.

2. Fold all E squares in half on one diagonal right side out; press. Set aside 14 for the Folded Square blocks.

3. Pin and machine-baste a folded E triangle on the A corner of each of 36 Red Delicious blocks to make Folded Red Delicious blocks, matching raw edges and referring to Figure 7.

Figure 7　　　　　**Figure 8**

4. Starting at the center of the E triangles, turn the folded edge back on itself approximately ½" and taper it out to the corners as shown in Figure 8. Press and hold in place with small dots of fabric glue.

5. Topstitch folded edges in place as shown in Figure 9.

Figure 9

COMPLETING THE FOLDED SQUARE BLOCKS

1. Pin and machine-baste a folded E triangle on one corner of each D square, matching raw edges, to complete 14 Folded Square blocks as shown in Figure 10.

Figure 10

2. Repeat steps 4 and 5 of Completing the Folded Red Delicious blocks to complete the blocks.

COMPLETING THE QUILT

1. Select four Folded Square blocks and four Red Delicious blocks. Alternate and join to make an X row as shown in Figure 11; press seams in one direction. Repeat to make two X rows.

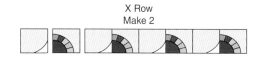

Figure 11

2. Select one each Folded Square and Red Delicious block and six Folded Red Delicious blocks. Arrange and join to make a Y row as shown in Figure 12; press seams in one direction. Repeat to make six Y rows.

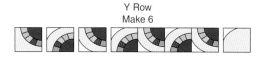

Figure 12

3. Arrange and join the rows referring to the Assembly Diagram for positioning; press seams in one direction.

4. Using diagonal seams, join the assorted F strips on short ends to make one long strip; subcut strip into four 64½" F strips.

5. Fold each F strip in half with wrong sides together along length; press.

6. Align, pin and baste raw edges of an F strip to the top and bottom, and then to opposite sides of the pieced center referring to Figure 13. **Note:** *The folded edge of these strips will face toward the quilt center and will remain loose.*

Figure 13

7. Join the G/H strips on short ends to make one long strip; press seams open. Subcut strip into two 64½" G strips and two 68½" H strips.
8. Sew a G strip to the top and bottom and H strips to opposite long sides; press seams toward G and H strips.
9. Create a quilt sandwich referring to Quilting Basics on page 62.

10. Quilt as desired.
11. Bind referring to Quilting Basics on page 62 to finish. ●

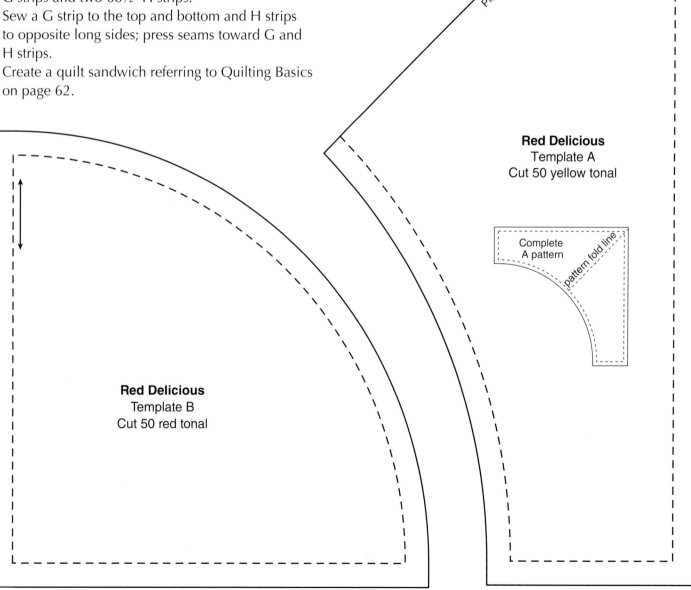

Red Delicious
Template A
Cut 50 yellow tonal

Place line on fold

Complete
A pattern

pattern fold line

Red Delicious
Template B
Cut 50 red tonal

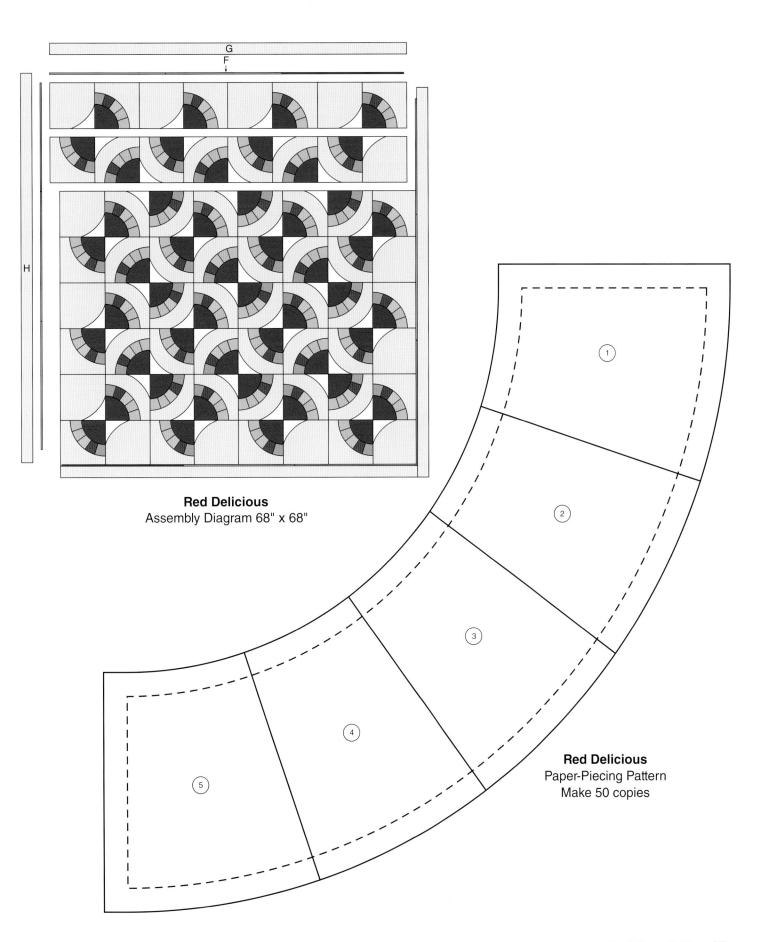

Red Delicious
Assembly Diagram 68" x 68"

Red Delicious
Paper-Piecing Pattern
Make 50 copies

Steppingstones

This quilted path leads to the forest—peaceful, serene and elegant!

Design by Tricia Lynn Maloney

Skill Level
Beginner

Finished Size
Quilt Size: 54" x 74"
Block Size: 10" x 10" finished
Number of Blocks: 35

MATERIALS

- 30 assorted 2½" x 42" precut tonal strips
- ½ yard each 6 assorted coordinating textural fabrics
- 7 assorted 2½" x 42" precut strips for binding
- Backing to size
- Batting to size
- Thread
- Basic sewing tools and supplies

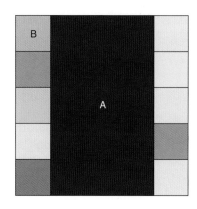

Steppingstones
10" x 10" Finished Block
Make 35

CUTTING

From assorted precut strips:
- Cut 2 (2½" x 21") strips from each precut strip for a total of 60 B strips.

From assorted textural fabrics:
- Cut 1 (10½" x 42") strip from each fabric.
  Subcut 6 (6½" x 10½") rectangles from each strip. Discard 1 rectangle for a total of 35 A rectangles.
- Cut 1 (2½" x 42") strip from each fabric.
  Subcut 2 (2½" x 10½") strips from each strip for a total of 12 C strips.
- Cut a total of 4 (2½") D squares.

COMPLETING THE BLOCKS

1. Select five different B strips and sew together along length to make a B strip set; press seams in one direction. Repeat to make a total of 12 B strip sets.
2. Subcut the B strip sets into a total of 82 (2½") B units referring to Figure 1; set aside 12 B units for Completing the Quilt.
3. Select two different B units and sew a unit to opposite sides of an A rectangle to complete one Steppingstones block as shown in Figure 2; press seams toward A.
4. Repeat step 3 to complete a total of 35 Steppingstones blocks.

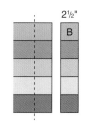

Figure 1

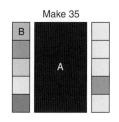

Make 35

Figure 2

COMPLETING THE QUILT

1. Select and join five Steppingstones blocks to make an X row, alternating the orientation of the blocks referring to Figure 3; press seams in one direction. Repeat to make a total of four X rows.

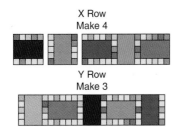

Figure 3

2. Repeat step 1 with five blocks, alternating the orientation of the blocks from those in the X row to complete a Y row, again referring to Figure 3; press seams in the opposite direction from the X rows. Repeat to make a total of three Y rows.

3. Referring to the Assembly Diagram for positioning of rows, join the X and Y rows, starting and ending with an X row; press seams in one direction.

4. Select and join two B units with three C strips to make the top strip as shown in Figure 4; press seams toward C strips. Repeat to make the bottom strip.

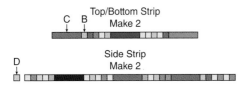

Figure 4

5. Sew the top strip to the top and bottom strip to the bottom of the pieced center; press seams toward the strips.

6. Join four B units with three C strips and add D to each end to make a side strip, again referring to Figure 4; press seams toward C strips. Repeat to make a second side strip.

7. Sew a side strip to opposite long sides of the pieced center to complete the quilt top; press seams toward side strips.

8. Create a quilt sandwich referring to Quilting Basics on page 62.

9. Quilt as desired.

10. Bind referring to Quilting Basics on page 62 to finish. ●

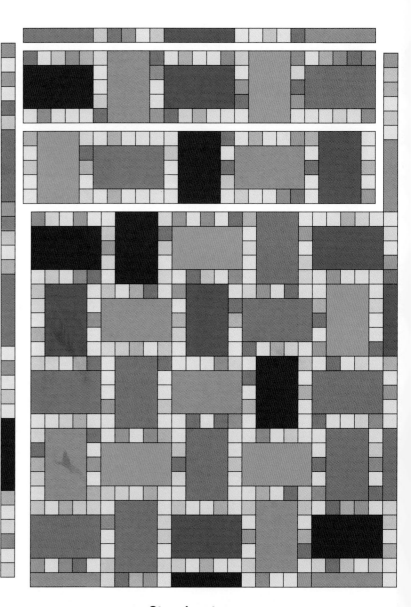

Steppingstones
Assembly Diagram 54" x 74"

Home Is Where the Quilt Is

Make this gorgeous classic quilt in any fabric collection. Make it your own.

Design by Wendy Sheppard

Skill Level
Beginner

Finished Size
Quilt Size: 45" x 56"
Block Size: 10½" x 10½" finished
Number of Blocks: 12

MATERIALS

- ¼ yard light gray tonal
- ¼ yard dark brown print
- ⅔ yard green print
- ⅔ yard dark gray print
- ⅔ yard cream tonal
- ¾ yard tan tonal
- 1¼ yards gold/green plaid
- Backing to size
- Batting to size
- Thread
- Basic sewing tools and supplies

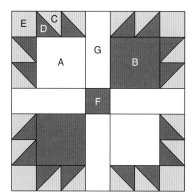

Green Bear Paw
10½" x 10½" Finished Block
Make 4

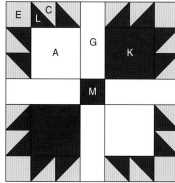

Dark Brown Bear Paw
10½" x 10½" Finished Block
Make 2

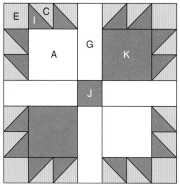

Dark Gray Bear Paw
10½" x 10½" Finished Block
Make 4

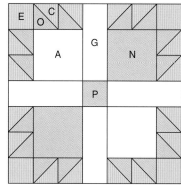

Light Gray Bear Paw
10½" x 10½" Finished Block
Make 2

CUTTING

From light gray tonal:
- Cut 1 (3½" x 42") strip.
  Subcut 4 (3½") N squares and 2 (2") P squares.
- Cut 1 (2⅜" x 42") strip.
  Subcut 16 (2⅜") O squares.

From dark brown print:
- Cut 1 (3½" x 42") strip.
  Subcut 4 (3½") K squares and 2 (2") M squares.
- Cut 1 (2⅜" x 42") strip.
  Subcut 16 (2⅜") L squares.

From green print:
- Cut 1 (3½" x 32") strip.
  Subcut 8 (3½") B squares and 4 (2") F squares.
- Cut 2 (2⅜" x 42") strips.
  Subcut 32 (2⅜") D squares.
- Cut 8 (1" x 42") strips.
  Subcut 8 (1" x 11") Q strips and 5 (1" x 33") R strips.
- Cut 3 (1" x 42") S strips.

From dark gray print:
- Cut 1 (3½" x 42") strip.
  Subcut 8 (3½") H squares and 4 (2") J squares.
- Cut 2 (2⅜" x 42") strips.
  Subcut 32 (2⅜") I squares.
- Cut 3 (2¼" x 42") T strips.
- Cut 2 (2¼' x 37½") U strips.

From cream tonal:
- Cut 2 (3½" x 42") strips.
  Subcut 24 (3½") A squares.
- Cut 6 (2" x 42") strips.
  Subcut 48 (2" x 5") G rectangles.

From tan tonal:
- Cut 3 (2" x 42") strips.
  Subcut 48 (2") E squares.
- Cut 6 (2⅜" x 42") strips.
  Subcut 96 (2⅜") C squares.

From gold/green plaid:
- Cut 5 (4½" x 42") V/W strips.
- Cut 6 (2¼" x 42") binding strips.

COMPLETING THE BLOCKS

1. Mark a diagonal line from corner to corner on the wrong side of all C squares.
2. Place a C square right sides together with a D square and stitch ¼" on each side of the marked line as shown in Figure 1.

Figure 1

3. Cut the stitched unit apart on the marked line to make two C-D units as shown in Figure 2; press units open with seams pressed toward D.

Figure 2

4. Repeat steps 2 and 3 with C and D squares to complete a total of 64 C-D units.
5. Repeat steps 2 and 3 with C and I to complete a total of 64 C-I units and with C and L and C and O to complete a total of 32 each C-L and C-O units referring to Figure 3.

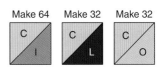

Figure 3

6. To complete one Green Bear Paw block, select 16 C-D units one F square, two each A and B squares, and four each E and G pieces.
7. Join two C-D units and then add A as shown in Figure 4; press seam to one side and then toward A.

Figure 4

8. Join two C-D units with E as shown in Figure 5; press seams toward E.

Figure 5

9. Sew the C-D-E unit to the C-D-A unit to complete one light corner unit as shown in Figure 6. Repeat to make a second light corner unit.

Figure 6

10. Repeat steps 7–9 with B instead of A to complete two dark corner units as shown in Figure 7.

Figure 7

11. Join one each light and dark corner unit with G to make a side row as shown in Figure 8; press seams toward G. Repeat to make a second side row.

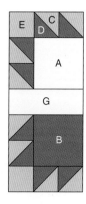

Figure 8   **Figure 9**

12. Sew G to opposite sides of F to make the center row as shown in Figure 9; press seams toward G.

13. Sew a side row to each long side of the center row to complete one Green Bear Paw block as shown in Figure 10; press seams toward the center row.

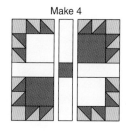

Make 4

Figure 10

14. Repeat steps 6–13 to complete a total of four Green Bear Paw blocks.

15. Repeat steps 6–13 with C-I units and A, E, H, G and J pieces to complete four Dark Gray Bear Paw blocks referring to Figure 11 and the block drawing.

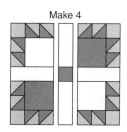

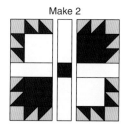

Make 4   Make 2

Figure 11   **Figure 12**

16. Repeat steps 6–13 with C-L units and A, E, G, K and M pieces to complete two Dark Brown Bear Paw blocks referring to Figure 12 and the block drawing.

17. Repeat steps 6-13 with C-O units and A, E, G, N and P pieces to complete two Light Gray Bear Paw blocks referring to Figure 13 and the block drawing.

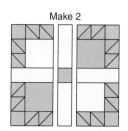

Make 2

Figure 13

COMPLETING THE QUILT

1. Arrange and join one each Green, Dark Brown and Dark Gray Bear Paw block with two Q strips to make a W row as shown in Figure 14; press seams toward Q strips.

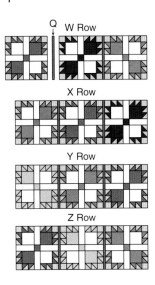

Figure 14

2. Arrange and join one each Dark Gray, Green and Dark Brown Bear Paw block with two Q strips to make an X row, again referring to Figure 14; press seams toward Q strips.

3. Arrange and join one each Light Gray, Dark Gray and Green Bear Paw block with two Q strips to make a Y row, again referring to Figure 14; press seams toward Q strips.

4. Arrange and join one each Green, Light Gray and Dark Gray Paw block with two Q strips to make a Z row, again referring to Figure 14; press seams toward Q strips.

5. Arrange and join the rows with the five R strips referring to the Assembly Diagram for positioning of rows; press seams toward R strips to complete the pieced center.

6. Join the S strips on short ends to make a long strip; press seams open. Subcut strip into two 45" S strips.

7. Sew an S strip to opposite long sides of the pieced center; press seams toward S strips.

8. Join the T strips on short ends to make a long strip; press seams open. Subcut strip into two 45" T strips.

9. Sew T strips to opposite long sides and U strips to the top and bottom of the pieced center; press seams toward T and U strips.

10. Join the V/W strips on short ends to make one long strip; press seams open. Subcut strip into two 48½" V strips and two 45½" W strips.

11. Sew V strips to opposite long sides and W strips to the top and bottom of the pieced center; press seams toward V and W strips to complete the quilt top.

12. Create a quilt sandwich referring to Quilting Basics on page 62.

13. Quilt as desired.

14. Bind referring to Quilting Basics on page 62 to finish. ●

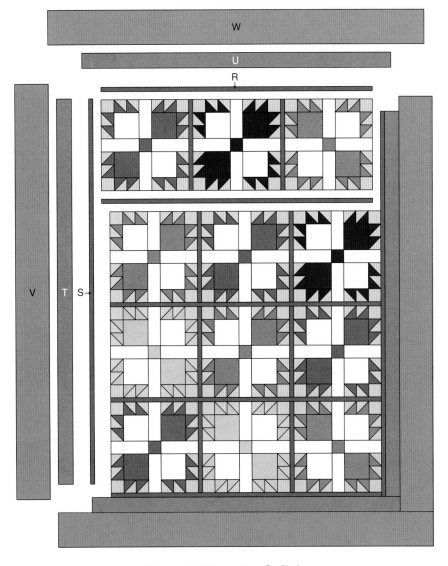

Home Is Where the Quilt Is
Assembly Diagram 45" x 56"

Woven Links

Play connect the pieces with this quilted puzzle. Imaginative color placement creates the optical illusion of weaving fabrics.

Design by Gina Gempesaw

Skill Level
Intermediate

Finished Size
Quilt Size: 63" x 75¾"
Block Size: 9" x 9" finished
Number of Blocks: 32

CUTTING

From green tonal:
- Cut 3 (6½" x 42") strips.
  Subcut 32 (3½" x 6½") C rectangles.
- Cut 3 (3½" x 42") strips.
  Subcut 32 (3½") G squares.

From teal tonal:
- Cut 3 (6½" x 42") strips.
  Subcut 32 (3½" x 6½") D rectangles.
- Cut 3 (3½" x 42") strips.
  Subcut 32 (3½") H squares.

From orange/purple tonal:
- Cut 3 (6½" x 42") strips.
  Subcut 32 (3½" x 6½") E rectangles.
- Cut 3 (3½" x 42") strips.
  Subcut 32 (3½") I squares.

From red/orange tonal:
- Cut 3 (6½" x 42") strips.
  Subcut 32 (3½" x 6½") F rectangles.
- Cut 3 (3½" x 42") strips.
  Subcut 32 (3½") J squares.

MATERIALS

- 1 yard green tonal
- 1 yard teal tonal
- 1 yard orange/purple tonal
- 1 yard red/orange tonal
- 2 yards yellow tonal
- 2¼ yards purple tonal
- Backing to size
- Batting to size
- Thread
- Basic sewing tools and supplies

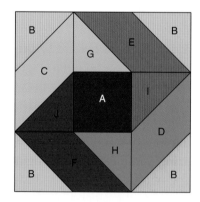

Links
9" x 9" Finished Block
Make 32

From yellow tonal:

- Cut 11 (3½" x 42") strips.
    Subcut 128 (3½") B squares.
- Cut 2 (14" x 42") strips.
    Subcut 4 (14") squares. Cut each square on both
    diagonals to make 16 K triangles.
    Subcut 2 (7¼") squares. Cut each square in half
    on 1 diagonal to make 4 L triangles.

From purple tonal:

- Cut 3 (3½" x 42") strips.
    Subcut 32 (3½") A squares.
- Cut 7 (6½" x 42") M/N strips.
- Cut 7 (2¼" x 42") binding strips.

COMPLETING THE LINKS BLOCKS

1. Draw a diagonal line from corner to corner on the
   wrong side of each B, G, H, I and J square.
2. Place a B square right sides together on the left end
   of a C rectangle and stitch on the marked line as
   shown in Figure 1; trim seam to ¼" and press B to
   the right side, again referring to Figure 1.

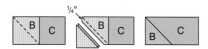

Figure 1

3. Repeat step 2 with B on the left end of each C, D, E
   and F rectangle as shown in Figure 2.

Figure 2

4. Repeat step 2 with a J square on the opposite end
   of each B-C unit, I on each B-D unit, G on each B-E
   unit and H on each B-F unit referring to Figure 3 to
   make 32 of each pieced unit.

Figure 3

5. To complete one Links block, select one A square
   and one each B-C-J, B-D-I, B-E-G and B-F-H unit.
6. Match the H end of a B-F-H unit right sides together
   on the bottom edge of A and stitch a partial seam
   as shown in Figure 4; press the stitched end of the
   seam toward A.

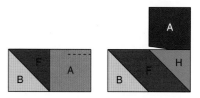

Figure 4

7. Sew a B-D-I unit to the right edge of the stitched unit as shown in Figure 5; press seam toward A.

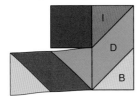

Figure 5

8. Sew a B-E-G unit to the top edge of the stitched unit as shown in Figure 6; press seam toward A.

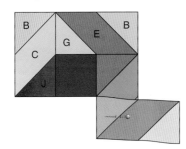

Figure 6

9. Pin the B-F-H unit out of the way, and add a B-C-J unit to the left edge of the stitched unit, as shown in Figure 6; press seam toward A.

10. Unpin the B-F-H unit and complete the seam between it and A and the B-C-J unit as shown in Figure 7 to complete one Links block; press seam toward A.

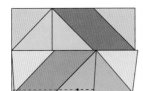

Figure 7

11. Repeat steps 5–10 to complete a total of 32 Links blocks.

COMPLETING THE QUILT

1. Referring to the Assembly Diagram, arrange and join the completed Links blocks in diagonal rows with the K and L triangles; press seams in adjoining rows in opposite directions.

2. Join the stitched diagonal rows to complete the pieced center; press seams in one direction.

3. Join the M/N strips on short ends to make one long strip; press seams open. Subcut strip into two 64¼" M strips and two 62½" N strips.

4. Sew M strips to opposite long sides and N strips to the top and bottom of the pieced center to complete the quilt top; press seams toward M and N strips.

5. Create a quilt sandwich referring to Quilting Basics on page 62.

6. Quilt as desired.

7. Bind referring to Quilting Basics on page 62 to finish. ●

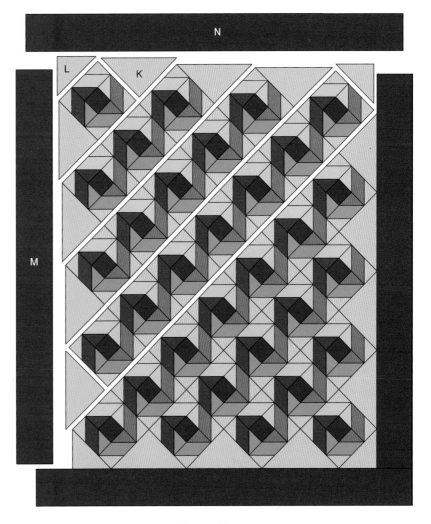

Woven Links
Assembly Diagram 63" x 75¾"

Garden Labyrinth

If you love formal gardens, you'll love this quilt.
It looks intricate, but it's easy to make!

Design by Sue Harvey & Sandy Boobar of Pine Tree Country Quilts

Skill Level
Confident Beginner

Finished Size
Quilt Size: 52" x 65"
Block Size: 11" x 11" finished
Number of Blocks: 12

CUTTING

From white/red print:
- Cut 4 (2½" x 42") G strips.

From red/black dot:
- Cut 1 (1½" x 42") strip.
  Subcut 12 (1½") H squares.
- Cut 6 (2¼" x 42") binding strips.

From white/gray print:
- Cut 2 (1½" x 42") B strips.
- Cut 3 (2½" x 42") C strips.
- Cut 3 (4½" x 42") strips.
  Subcut 48 (2½" x 4½") D rectangles.

From red pebble print:
- Cut 9 (1½" x 42") A strips.
- Cut 1 (2½" x 42") strip.
  Subcut 6 (2½") J squares.
- Cut 3 (2½" x 42") K strips.
- Cut 2 (2½" x 41½") L strips.

Labyrinth
11" x 11" Finished Block
Make 12

From black print:
- Cut 4 (2½" x 42") E strips.
- Cut 2 (4½" x 42") strips.
  Subcut 48 (1½" x 4½") F strips.
- Cut 6 (2½" x 42") strips.
  Subcut 17 (2½" x 11½") I strips.

From black flower print:
- Cut 6 (6" x 42") M/N strips.

COMPLETING THE BLOCKS

1. Sew an A strip to a B strip with right sides together along length to make an A-B strip set; press seam toward A. Repeat to make a second strip set. Repeat with A and C strips to make three A-C strip sets.

2. Subcut the A-B strip sets into 48 (1½") A-B units and the A-C strip sets into 48 (2½") A-C units referring to Figure 1.

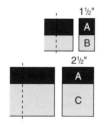

Figure 1

3. Sew an A strip between two E strips to make an A-E strip set; press seams toward E strips. Repeat to make a second A-E strip set. Repeat with A and G strips to make two A-G strip sets, pressing seams toward the A strips.

4. Subcut the A-E strip sets into 48 (1½") A-E units and the A-G strip sets into 48 (1½") A-G units referring to Figure 2.

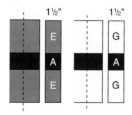

Figure 2

5. Sew an A-B unit to the A edge of an A-C unit and add a D rectangle to one long edge as shown in Figure 3; press seams toward the A-C unit and D.

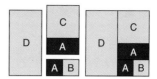

Figure 3

6. Sew an F strip to the A-B-D edge and an A-E unit to the adjacent edge of the pieced unit to complete a corner unit as shown in Figure 4; press seams toward the F strip and A-E unit.

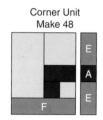

Corner Unit
Make 48

Figure 4

7. Repeat steps 5 and 6 to complete a total of 48 corner units.

8. To piece one Labyrinth block, sew an A-G unit between two corner units to make the top row as shown in Figure 5; press seams toward the corner units. Repeat to make the bottom row.

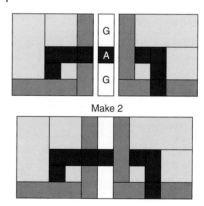

Make 2

Figure 5

9. Sew an H square between two A-G units to make the center row as shown in Figure 6; press seams toward H.

Figure 6

10. Sew the center row between the top and bottom rows to complete one Labyrinth block as shown in Figure 7; press seams toward the top and bottom rows.

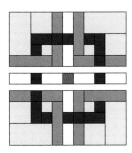

Figure 7

11. Repeat steps 8–10 to complete a total of 12 Labyrinth blocks.

COMPLETING THE QUILT

1. Join three Labyrinth blocks with two I strips to make a block row as shown in Figure 8; press seams toward I strips. Repeat to make a total of four block rows.

2. Join three I strips with two J squares to make a sashing row, again referring to Figure 8; press seams toward I strips. Repeat to make a total of three sashing rows.

Make 4

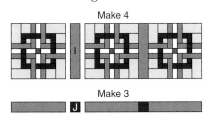

Make 3

Figure 8

3. Join the block rows with the sashing rows to complete the quilt center referring to the Assembly Diagram for positioning; press seams toward sashing rows.

4. Join the K strips on short ends to make a long strip; press seams open. Subcut strip into two 50½" K strips.

5. Sew the K strips to opposite long sides and L strips to the top and bottom of the pieced center; press seams toward K and L strips.

6. Join the M/N strips on short ends to make a long strip; press seams open. Subcut strip into two 54½" M strips and two 52½" N strips.

7. Sew M strips to opposite long sides and N strips to the top and bottom of the pieced center to complete the quilt top; press seams toward M and N strips.

8. Create a quilt sandwich referring to Quilting Basics on page 62.

9. Quilt as desired.

10. Bind referring to Quilting Basics on page 62 to finish. ●

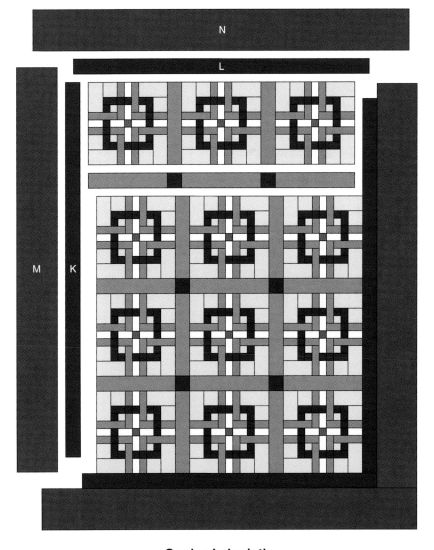

Garden Labyrinth
Assembly Diagram 52" x 65"

Batiks Squared

It's time to put a dent in your batik stash. This quilt does the trick.

Design by Jill Reber

Skill Level
Beginner

Finished Size
Quilt Size: 74" x 98"
Block Size: 6" x 6" finished
Number of Blocks: 64

MATERIALS

- ⅝ yard each 8 batiks
- 1¾ yards dark-colored batik
- 2⅝ yards print batik
- Backing to size
- Batting to size
- Thread
- Basic sewing tools and supplies

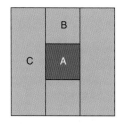

Batik Five-Patch
6" x 6" Finished Block
Make 64

CUTTING

From each of 8 batiks:
- Cut 5 (2½" by fabric width) A, B, E, F and H strips.
    Subcut A into 1 (2½" x 21") strip.
    Subcut each E strip into 12 (2½" x 4½")
    E rectangles for a total of 96 rectangles.
    Subcut each F strip into 12 (2½") F squares
    for a total of 96 squares.
    Subcut each H strip into 5 (2½") H squares.
    Discard 5 for a total of 35 H squares.
- Cut 1 (6½" by fabric width) strip.
    Subcut each strip into 12 (2½" x 6½")
    C rectangles for a total of 128 C rectangles.

From dark-colored batik:
- Cut 6 (2½" by fabric width) strips.
    Subcut into 96 (2½") D squares.
- Cut 4 (10½" by fabric width) strips.
    Subcut into 58 (2½" x 10½") G rectangles.

From print batik:
- Cut 6 (6½" by fabric width) I/J strips from print batik.
- Cut 2 (6½" x 26½") L strips and 2 (6½" x 38½")
    K strips from print batik.
- Cut 9 (2¼" by fabric width) binding strips.

COMPLETING THE BLOCKS

1. Select one 2½" x 21" A strip. Cut one B strip to make
    two 2½" x 21" B strips.
2. Sew the A strip between the two B strips to make an
    A-B strip; press seams toward B strips.

3. Subcut the A-B strip into one set of eight 2½" A-B units as shown in Figure 1.

Figure 1

4. Repeat steps 1–3 to make eight different A-B sets.
5. To complete one matching set of eight Batik Five-Patch blocks, select one set of eight matching A-B units and 16 C rectangles from the same fabric as B.
6. Sew a C rectangle to opposite sides of each A-B unit to complete eight matching blocks; press seams toward C rectangles.
7. Repeat steps 1–6 to complete eight sets of matching blocks to total 64 blocks.

COMPLETING THE PIECED CENTER

1. Select and set aside 40 Batik Five-Patch blocks for borders.
2. Select four each E rectangles and F squares from one fabric and four D squares from another fabric.
3. Sew a D square between two F squares to make a D-F unit as shown in Figure 2; press seams toward F squares. Repeat to make two D-F units.

     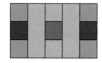

Figure 2   **Figure 3**

4. Sew a D-F unit to the C sides of one Batik Five-Patch block as shown in Figure 3; press seams toward C.
5. Sew a D square between two E rectangles to make a D-E unit as shown in Figure 4; press seams toward E rectangles. Repeat to make two D-E units.

Figure 4

6. Sew a D-E unit to the remaining sides of the Batik Five-Patch block to complete a block unit as shown in Figure 5; press seams toward D-E units.

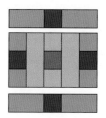

Figure 5

7. Repeat steps 2–6 to complete 24 block units.
8. Join four block units with five G strips to make a block row, sewing G to the D-F sides of the blocks as shown in Figure 6; press seams toward G strips. Repeat to make six block rows.

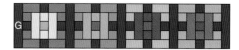

Figure 6

9. Join four G strips with five H squares to make a sashing row as shown in Figure 7; press seams toward G strips. Repeat to make seven sashing rows.

Make 7

Figure 7

10. Join the block rows with the sashing rows, beginning and ending with sashing rows; press seams toward sashing rows to complete the pieced center.

COMPLETING THE QUILT

1. Join the I/J strips on short ends to make one long strip; press seams open. Subcut strips into two 62½" I strips and two 50½" J strips.
2. Sew the B side of one Batik Five-Patch block to each end of each I strip as shown in Figure 8; press seams toward I strips. Repeat to make two I/block strips.

Make 2

Make 2

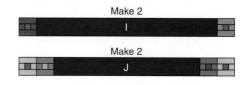

Figure 8

3. Repeat step 1 with two Batik Five-Patch blocks on each end of each J strip to make two J/block strips, again referring to Figure 8.

4. Join one each I/block strip and J/block strip along length to make a side strip; press seams toward I/block strip. Repeat to make two side strips.

5. Sew a side strip to opposite long sides of the pieced center referring to the Assembly Diagram for positioning; press seams toward side strips.

6. Join three blocks on the C sides; press seams in one direction. Repeat to make two three-block units and two four-block units as shown in Figure 9.

Make 2

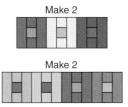

Make 2

Figure 9

7. Sew a three-block unit to each end of each K strip and a four-block unit to each end of each L strip to make two each K/block and L/block strips as shown in Figure 10; press seams toward strips.

Make 2

K

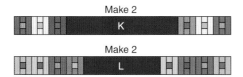

Make 2

L

Figure 10

8. Join one each K/block strip and L/block strip to make the top strip as shown in Figure 11; press seam toward the L/block strip. Repeat to make the bottom strip.

Figure 11

9. Sew the top and bottom strips to the top and bottom of the pieced top referring to the Assembly Diagram to complete the pieced top; press seams toward strips.

10. Create a quilt sandwich referring to Quilting Basics on page 62.

11. Quilt as desired.

12. Bind referring to Quilting Basics on page 62 to finish. ●

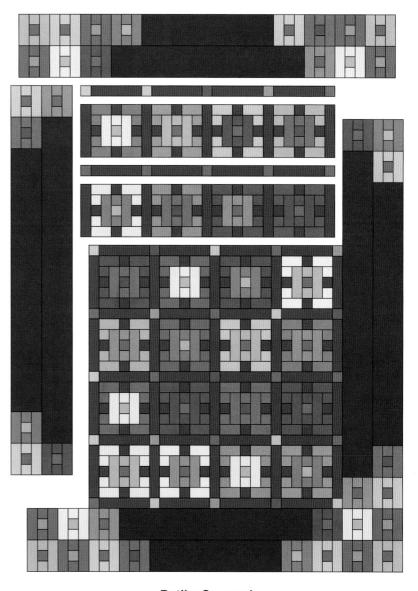

Batiks Squared
Assembly Diagram 74" x 98"

Puzzle Hearts

Paper-pieced hearts and smaller pieced and appliquéd units make up the blocks in this scrappy quilt.

Design by Jodi G. Warner

Skill Level
Advanced

Finished Size
Quilt Size: 51" x 61¾"
Block Sizes: 7" x 10¾" finished and 3¾" x 10¾" finished
Number of Blocks: 20 and 20

MATERIALS

- 5 scraps each:
  - violet   teal/turquoise
  - yellow   pink
- 5 fat eighths each pink and violet
- 5 pink scraps
- 5 sets 9 varied scraps:
  - rose   pink   deep teal
  - teal   orange
  - violet   deep pink
- 5 fat eighths each yellow
- 5 fat eighths each turquoise/teal
- ¼ yard each 5 cream mini prints
- ⅓ yard each 5 violet fabrics
- ⅓ yard each 5 bright pink fabrics
- ⅝ yard each 5 yellow fabrics
- ⅝ yard deep red tonal
- 1⅜ yards yellow print
- Backing to size
- Batting to size
- Thread
- ¼ yard 18"-wide lightweight paper-backed fusible web
- Basic sewing tools and supplies

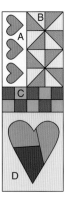

Small Heart
3¾" x 10¾" Finished Block
Make 20

Large Heart
7" x 10¾" Finished Block
Make 20

CUTTING

Use provided patterns found on pages 54–56 for paper-piecing and appliqué to make templates for your favorite techniques. Cut from fabric as indicated on patterns and in instructions.

From each of 5 pink and violet fat eighths:
- Cut 2 (1¼" x 21") strips to total 10 C strips.

From each of 5 yellow fat eighths:
- Cut 4 (4") squares to total 20 B squares.

From each of 5 turquoise/teal fat eighths:
- Cut 4 (4") squares to total 20 B squares.

From each of 5 cream mini prints:
- Cut 1 (2" x 42") strip.
  Subcut 4 (2" x 5") rectangles to total 20 A rectangles.
- Cut 2 (2⅛" x 42") strips.
  Subcut 28 (2⅛") squares. Cut each square in half on 1 diagonal to make 56 triangles for a total of 280 H triangles.

From each of 5 violet fabrics:

- Cut 1 (3" x 42") strip.
  Subcut 28 (1½" x 3") rectangles to total 140 G rectangles.

From each of 5 bright pink fabrics:

- Cut 1 (1¾" x 42") strip.
  Subcut 4 (1¾" x 3½") rectangles to total 20 F rectangles.

From each of 5 yellow fabrics:

- Cut 1 (5¼" x 42") strip.
  Subcut 4 (4¼" x 5¼") rectangles to total 20 D rectangles.
- Cut 1 (1¾" x 42") strip.
  Subcut 4 (1¾" x 2") rectangles to total 20 E rectangles.

From deep red tonal:

- Cut 5 (1½" x 42) I/J strips.

From yellow print:

- Cut 6 (3½" x 42") K/L strips.
- Cut 250" of 2¼"-wide bias strips for quilt binding.

COMPLETING THE MINI HEART PANELS

1. Transfer heart positions to the right side of each A piece using a water-erasable marker or chalk pencil and the positioning pattern given on page 54.
2. Use mini heart template to trace 60 mini hearts onto the paper side of the fusible web; cut out shapes, leaving a margin around each one.
3. Fuse 12 mini heart shapes to the wrong side of each of five pink fabric scraps; cut out shapes on traced lines. Remove paper backing.
4. Arrange and fuse three same-fabric hearts on each A piece using transfer lines as guides for positioning.
5. Blanket-stitch around each heart shape by hand or machine using thread to match fabrics to complete the 20 mini heart panels.

COMPLETING THE PINWHEEL PANELS

1. Make 20 copies of the Section 1 pattern.
2. Layer a yellow B, right side up; a turquoise B, right side down; and a paper section 1 pattern, print side up. Pin layers together securely.

3. Stitch on all dashed lines; rotary-cut apart exactly on solid lines. Press half-square triangle units open with seam toward turquoise triangles to make eight B units as shown in Figure 1. Repeat with all squares to make 20 sets of eight same fabric B units.

Figure 1　　　　**Figure 2**

4. Join four same-fabric B units to make a pinwheel unit as shown in Figure 2; press seams in rows in opposite directions and in one direction on a completed pinwheel unit. Repeat to make 40 pinwheel units. Trim each pinwheel unit to 2¾" x 2¾".
5. Join two same-fabric pinwheel units to complete a pinwheel panel as shown in Figure 3; press seam in one direction. Repeat to make 20 pinwheel panels. Remove paper patterns.

Figure 3

COMPLETING THE CHECKERBOARD PANELS

1. Join one each pink and violet C strip with right sides together along length to make a C strip set; press seams toward violet side. Make two strip sets.
2. Subcut strip sets into 20 (1¼") C units as shown in Figure 4. Set aside extra strip set length for use in another project.

Figure 4　　　　**Figure 5**

3. Join five C units to make a checkerboard panel as shown in Figure 5; press seams in one direction. Repeat to make four matching panels.
4. Repeat steps 1–3 to make four more matching sets of panels from the remaining pink/violet C strips to total 20 checkerboard panels.

COMPLETING THE SCRAPPY HEART PANELS

1. Make 21 copies of Section 2 pattern.
2. Set machine stitch length to 25 stitches per inch or 1.5. To paper piece, cut up one Section 2 pattern to make three different templates; mark the piece number and color on each one.
3. Cut out shapes from violet, teal/turquoise and pink scraps using templates, adding a ¼" seam allowance all around when cutting. Cut four matching sets of pieces from each of the five scraps in each color.
4. Select an uncut Section 2 pattern. With printed side down, pin piece 1 over the piece 1 area on the paper piece, holding the paper up to the light to be sure that piece 1 extends beyond the piece 1 area all around as shown in Figure 6.

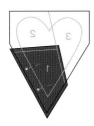

Figure 6

5. Pin piece 2 to piece 1 along the 1–2 line as shown in Figure 7.

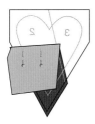

Figure 7

6. Turn the paper over and stitch on the line between areas 1 and 2 as shown in Figure 8.

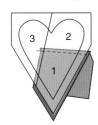

Figure 8

7. Turn paper over and press piece 2 to the right side as shown in Figure 9.

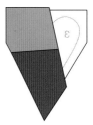

Figure 9

8. Repeat steps 5–7 with piece 3 to complete the pieced section as shown in Figure 10.

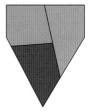

Figure 10

9. Cut out heart shape from the paper-pieced unit adding a ¼" seam allowance all around when cutting; trim away paper pattern in the seam allowance area only.
10. Turn edges of heart shape to the wrong side along edge of paper; press firmly. Remove paper pattern; baste turned-under edges to hold.
11. Center the heart shape on a D piece and appliqué by hand or machine to complete a scrappy heart panel referring to Figure 11 for placement.

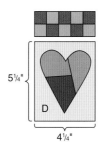

Figure 11

12. Repeat steps 3–11 to make five sets of four same-fabric scrappy heart panels to total 20 panels.

COMPLETING THE SMALL HEART BLOCKS

1. Sew a mini heart panel to the left side of a pinwheel panel as shown in Figure 12; press seam toward the mini heart panel.

Figure 12

2. Sew a checkerboard panel to the top edge of a scrappy heart panel, again referring to Figure 11; press seam toward the scrappy heart panel.

3. Join the two sections referring to the block drawing to complete one Small Heart block; press seam toward checkerboard panel.

4. Repeat steps 1–3 to complete 20 Small Heart blocks.

COMPLETING THE CRAZY-PATCH PANELS

1. Complete five sets of four identical Section 4 panels using pattern given and referring to the paper-piecing instructions given in steps 2–8 for Completing the Scrappy Heart Panels and referring to Figure 13.

Figure 3

2. When panels are complete, remove paper.

COMPLETING THE LARGE HEART PANELS

1. Make 21 copies of Section 3 pattern.

2. Select four same-fabric E and F pieces. Join along short ends to make a combo-patch as shown in Figure 14; press seams toward pink fabrics.

Figure 14

3. Select fabrics to match the stitched E-F combo-patch, one violet fabric and the red mottled.

4. Using a Section 3 pattern and referring to steps 2–8 in Completing the Scrappy Heart Panels for paper-piecing instructions and to Figure 15 for color placement, complete four identical large heart panels. When stitching is complete, remove paper.

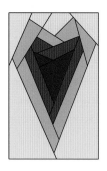

Figure 15

5. Repeat steps 2–4 to complete five sets of four identical large heart panels.

COMPLETING THE FLYING GEESE PANELS

1. Make 21 copies of Section 5 pattern.

2. Select seven same-fabric G pieces and 14 same-fabric H triangles.

3. Using the Section 5 paper-piecing patterns and referring to steps 2–8 in the Completing the Scrappy Heart Panels for paper-piecing instructions, complete one flying geese panel as shown in Figure 16.

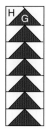

Figure 16

4. Repeat steps 2 and 3 to complete four sets of five same-fabric flying geese panels.

5. Remove paper when panels are complete.

COMPLETING THE LARGE HEART BLOCKS

1. Sew a crazy-patch panel to the right side edge of one large heart panel; press seam toward the large heart panel.
2. Sew a flying geese panel to the bottom of the stitched unit to complete one Large Heart block referring to the block drawing for positioning of the panel; press seam away from the flying geese panel.
3. Repeat steps 1 and 2 to complete 20 Large Heart blocks.

COMPLETING THE QUILT

1. Beginning with a Small Heart Block, join four each Small Heart and Large Heart blocks to make an X row referring to Figure 17; press seams toward Large Heart blocks. Repeat to make three X rows.

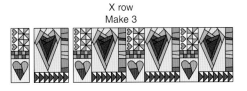

X row
Make 3

Figure 17

2. Repeat step 1 except begin with a Large Heart Block and join four each Large Heart and Small Heart blocks to make a Y row as shown in Figure 18; press seams toward Large Heart blocks. Repeat to make two Y rows.

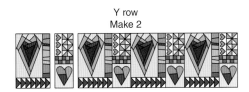

Y row
Make 2

Figure 18

3. Beginning with an X row, join the X and Y rows referring to the Placement Diagram for positioning; press seams in one direction to complete the pieced center.
4. Join the I/J strips on short ends to make one long strip; press seams open. Subcut strip into two 54¼" I strips and two 45½" J strips.

5. Sew an I strip to opposite long sides and J strips to the top and bottom of the pieced center; press seams toward I and J strips.
6. Join the K/L strips on short ends to make one long strip; press seams open. Subcut strip into two 56¼" K strips and two 51½" L strips.
7. Sew a K strip to opposite long sides and L strips to the top and bottom of the pieced center; press seams toward K and L strips to complete the pieced top.
8. Create a quilt sandwich referring to Quilting Basics on page 62.
9. Quilt as desired.
10. Bind referring to Quilting Basics on page 62 to finish. ●

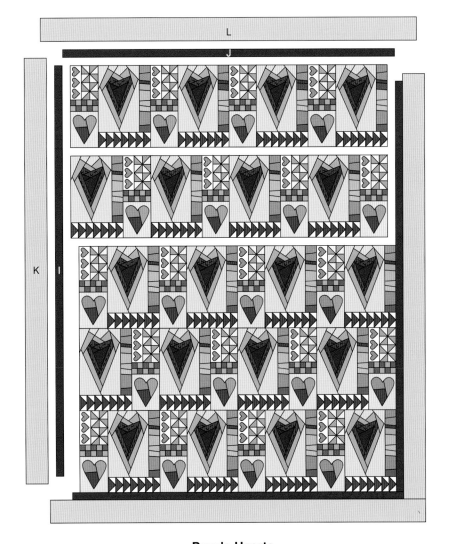

Puzzle Hearts
Assembly Diagram 51" x 61¾"

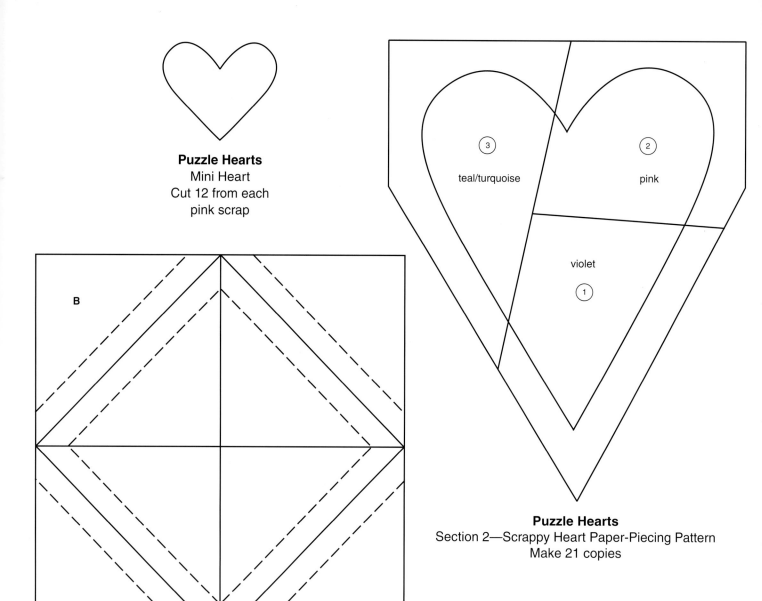

Puzzle Hearts
Mini Heart
Cut 12 from each
pink scrap

Puzzle Hearts
Section 2—Scrappy Heart Paper-Piecing Pattern
Make 21 copies

teal/turquoise

pink

violet

B

Puzzle Hearts
Section 1—Half-Square Triangles Pattern
Make 20 (each pattern makes 8 triangle units
to complete 2 pinwheel panels)

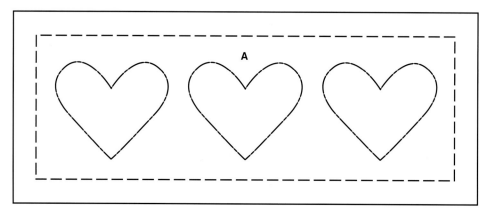

A

Puzzle Hearts
Mini Heart Positioning Pattern

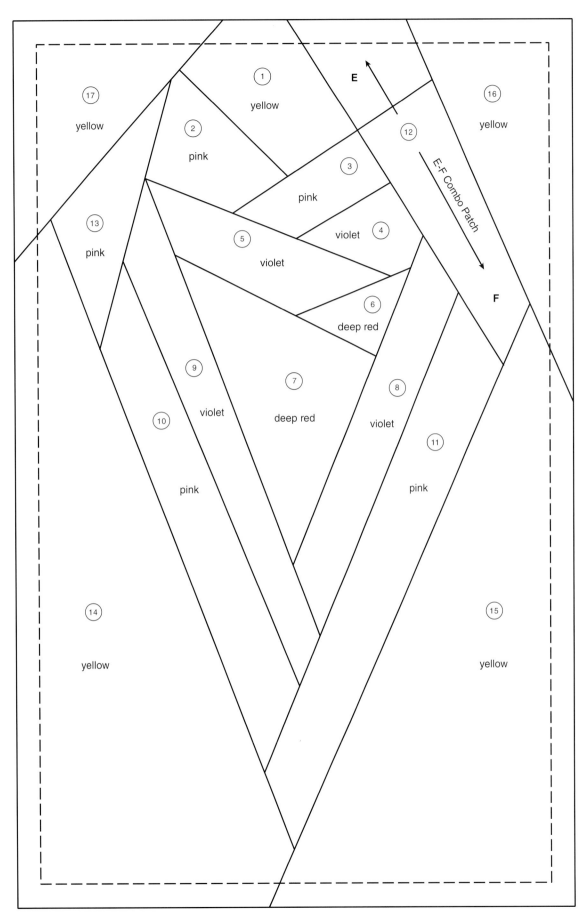

Puzzle Hearts
Section 3—Large Heart Paper-Piecing Pattern
Make 21 copies

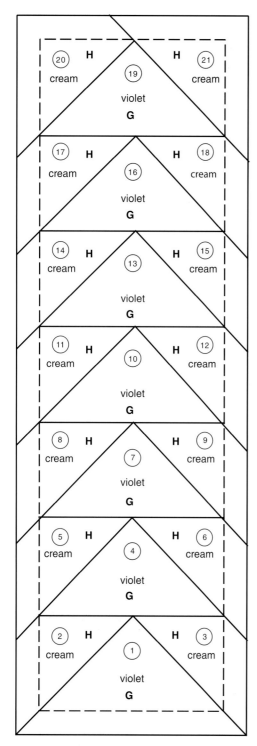

Puzzle Hearts
Section 5—Flying Geese Panel
Paper-Piecing Pattern
Make 21 copies

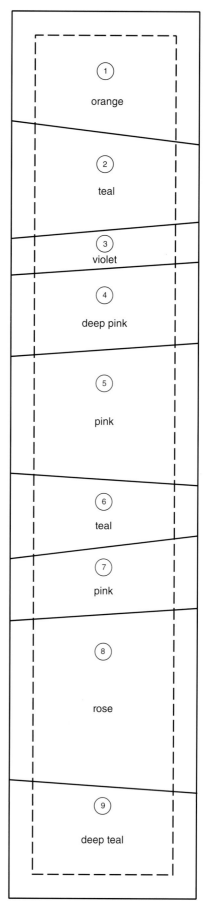

Puzzle Hearts
Section 4—Crazy-Patch Panel
Paper-Piecing Pattern
Make 21 copies

Sweet Bouquets

The interesting interplay of tonals, prints and solids creates a quilt that's sweet and a little bit sassy.

Designed & Quilted by Wendy Sheppard

Skill Level
Intermediate

Finished Size
Quilt Size: 41" x 53"
Block Size: 6" x 6" finished
Number of Blocks: 35

MATERIALS

- ¾ yard lavender tonal
- ¾ yard light green tonal
- ⅞ yard yellow dot
- ⅞ yard purple tonal
- 1⅝ yards cream floral
- Backing to size
- Batting to size
- Thread
- Template material
- Basic sewing tools and supplies

CUTTING

Prepare templates for E, I, F/FR and J using patterns found on page 60; cut from fabrics as directed on each pattern piece.

From lavender tonal:

- Cut 6 (1½" x 42") D strips.
- Cut 3 (2" x 42") M strips.
- Cut 2 (2" x 34½") N strips.

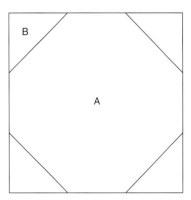

Cream Snowball
6" x 6" Finished Block
Make 9

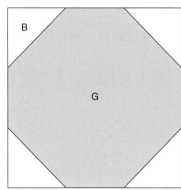

Green Snowball
6" x 6" Finished Block
Make 8

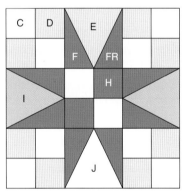

Garden Patch 1
6" x 6" Finished Block
Make 2

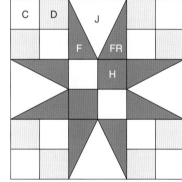

Garden Patch 2
6" x 6" Finished Block
Make 4

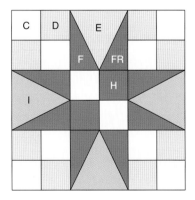

Garden Patch 3
6" x 6" Finished Block
Make 4

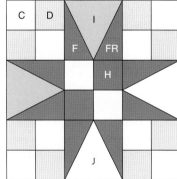

Garden Patch 4
6" x 6" Finished Block
Make 8

From light green tonal:
- Cut 2 (6½" x 42") strips.
  Subcut 8 (6½") G squares.

From yellow dot:
- Cut 5 (2½" x 42") strips.
  Subcut 68 (2½") B squares.
- Cut 8 (1½" x 42") C strips.

From purple tonal:
- Cut 2 (1½" x 42") H strips.
- Cut 2 (1" x 30½") K strips.
- Cut 3 (1" x 42") L strips.

From cream floral:
- Cut 2 (6½" x 42") strips.
  Subcut 9 (6½") A squares.
- Cut 2 (4" x 34½") O strips.
- Cut 3 (4" x 42") P strips.
- Cut 5 (2¼" x 42") binding strips.

COMPLETING THE SNOWBALL BLOCKS

1. Mark a diagonal line from corner to corner on the wrong side of each B square.
2. To complete one Cream Snowball block, place a marked B square on each corner of an A square and stitch on the marked lines as shown in Figure 1.

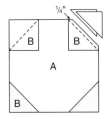 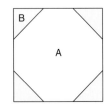

Figure 1   **Figure 2**

3. Trim the seam allowance to ¼" and press B pieces to the right side to complete one Cream Snowball block referring to Figure 2.
4. Repeat steps 2 and 3 to complete a total of nine Cream Snowball blocks.
5. Repeat steps 2 and 3 with B and G squares to complete a total of eight Green Snowball blocks referring to the block drawing.

COMPLETING THE GARDEN PATCH BLOCKS

1. Sew a C strip to a D strip with right sides together along length to make a C-D strip set; press seam toward D. Repeat to make a total of six C-D strip sets.
2. Subcut the C-D strip sets into 144 (1½") C-D units as shown in Figure 3.

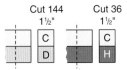

Figure 3   **Figure 4**

3. Join two C-D units to complete a corner unit as shown in Figure 4; press seam to one side. Repeat to make a total of 72 corner units.
4. Repeat step 1 with C and H strips to make two C-H strip sets; subcut strips into 36 (1½") C-H units, again referring to Figure 3.
5. Join two C-H units to make a center unit as shown in Figure 5; press seam to one side. Repeat to make a total of 18 center units.

          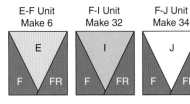

Figure 5   **Figure 6**

6. Sew F and FR to E to make six E-F units as shown in Figure 6; press seams away from E.
7. Sew F and FR to I to make 32 F-I units, again referring to Figure 6; press seams away from I.
8. Sew F and FR to J to make 34 F-J units, again referring to Figure 6; press seams away from J.
9. To complete one Garden Patch 1 block, select one center unit, four corner units, two F-I units and one each E-F and F-J unit.
10. Sew an E-F unit between two corner units to make the top row as shown in Figure 7; press seams toward the corner units.

Figure 7

11. Sew the center unit between two F-I units to make the center row as shown in Figure 8; press seam toward the center unit.

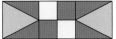

Figure 8

Figure 9

12. Sew the F-J unit between two corner units to make the bottom row referring to Figure 9; press seams toward the corner units.

13. Sew the center row between the top and bottom rows to complete the Garden Patch 1 block referring to Figure 10; press seams away from the center row.

14. Repeat steps 9–13 to complete a second Garden Patch 1 block.

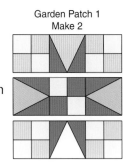

Garden Patch 1
Make 2

Figure 10

15. Select four corner units, four F-J units and one center unit to complete one Garden Patch 2 block referring to steps 9–13 and Figure 11. Repeat to make a total of four Garden Patch 2 blocks.

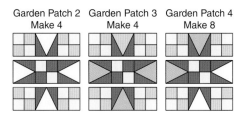

Garden Patch 2
Make 4

Garden Patch 3
Make 4

Garden Patch 4
Make 8

Figure 11

16. Select four corner units, one center unit, one E-F unit and three F-I units to complete one Garden Patch 3 block, again referring to steps 9–13 and Figure 11. Repeat to make a total of four Garden Patch 3 blocks.

17. Select four corner units, one center unit and two each F-I and F-J units to complete one Garden Patch 4 block, again referring to steps 9–13 and Figure 11. Repeat to make a total of eight Garden Patch 4 blocks.

COMPLETING THE QUILT

1. Select and join one Garden Patch 1 block and two each Green Snowball and Garden Patch 3 blocks to make a W row as shown in Figure 12; press seams toward the Green Snowball blocks. Repeat to make a second W row.

2. Select and join one Cream Snowball block and two each Green Snowball and Garden Patch 4 blocks to make an X row, again referring to Figure 12; press seams away from the Garden Patch 4 blocks. Repeat to make a second X row.

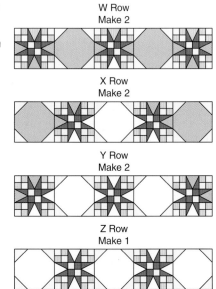

W Row
Make 2

X Row
Make 2

Y Row
Make 2

Z Row
Make 1

Figure 12

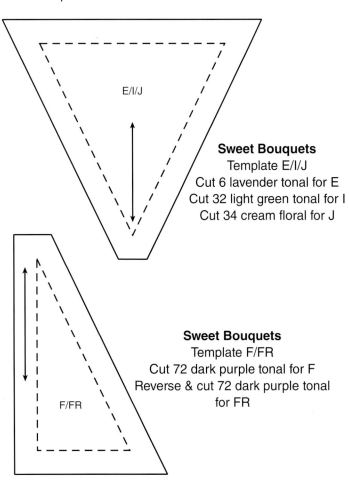

E/I/J

Sweet Bouquets
Template E/I/J
Cut 6 lavender tonal for E
Cut 32 light green tonal for I
Cut 34 cream floral for J

Sweet Bouquets
Template F/FR
Cut 72 dark purple tonal for F
Reverse & cut 72 dark purple tonal for FR

F/FR

3. Select and join one Garden Patch 2 block and two each Cream Snowball and Garden Patch 4 blocks to make a Y row, again referring to Figure 12; press seams toward the Cream Snowball blocks. Repeat to make a second Y row.

4. Select two Garden Patch 2 blocks and three Cream Snowball blocks to make a Z row, again referring to Figure 12; press seams toward the Cream Snowball blocks.

5. Sew a Y row to opposite sides of the Z row; add an X row to the Y rows and then a W row to the X rows to complete the pieced center referring to Figure 13; press seams in one direction.

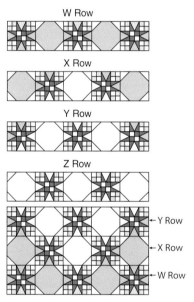

Figure 13

6. Sew a K strip to the top and bottom of the pieced center; press seams toward K strips.

7. Join the L strips on the short ends to make one long strip; press seams open. Subcut strip into two 43½" L strips. **Note:** *If your fabric is 43½" wide, no piecing will be necessary for these strips.*

8. Sew an L strip to opposite long sides of the pieced center; press seams toward L strips.

9. Join the M strips on the short ends to make one long strip; press seams open. Subcut strip into two 43½" M strips. **Note:** *If your fabric is 43½" wide, no piecing will be necessary for these strips.*

10. Sew an M strip to opposite long sides and N strips to the top and bottom of the pieced center; press seams toward M and N strips.

11. Sew an O strip to the top and bottom of the pieced center; press seams toward O strips.

12. Join the P strips on the short ends to make one long strip; press seams open. Subcut strip into two 53½" P strips.

13. Sew a P strip to opposite long sides of the pieced center; press seams toward P strips.

14. Create a quilt sandwich referring to Quilting Basics on page 62.

15. Quilt as desired.

16. Bind referring to Quilting Basics on page 62 to finish. ●

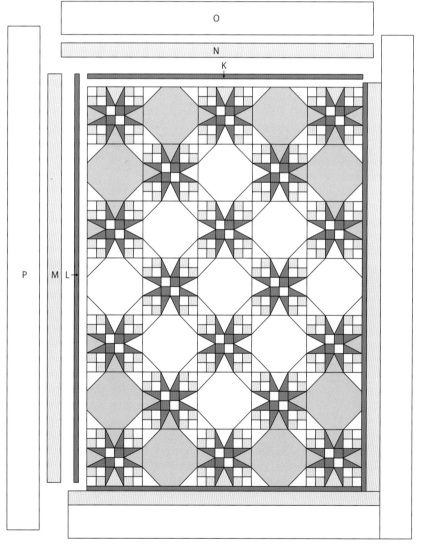

Sweet Bouquets
Assembly Diagram 41" x 53"

Quilting Basics

The following is a reference guide. For more information, consult a comprehensive quilting book.

ALWAYS:

- Read through the entire pattern before you begin your project.
- Purchase quality, 100 percent cotton fabrics.
- When considering prewashing, do so with ALL of the fabrics being used. Generally, prewashing is not required in quilting.
- Use ¼" seam allowance for all stitching unless otherwise instructed.
- Use a short-to-medium stitch length.
- Make sure your seams are accurate.

QUILTING TOOLS & SUPPLIES

- Rotary cutter and mat
- Scissors for paper and fabric
- Nonslip quilting rulers
- Marking tools
- Sewing machine
- Sewing machine feet:
- ¼" seaming foot (for piecing)
- Walking or even-feed foot (for piecing or quilting)
- Darning or free-motion foot (for free-motion quilting)
- Quilting hand-sewing needles
- Straight pins
- Curved safety pins for basting
- Seam ripper
- Iron and ironing surface

BASIC TECHNIQUES
Appliqué

FUSIBLE APPLIQUÉ

All templates are reversed for use with this technique.

1. Trace the instructed number of templates ¼" apart onto the paper side of paper-backed fusible web. Cut apart the templates, leaving a margin around each, and fuse to the wrong side of the fabric following fusible web manufacturer's instructions.
2. Cut the appliqué pieces out on the traced lines, remove paper backing and fuse to the background referring to the appliqué motif given.
3. Finish appliqué raw edges with a straight, satin, blanket, zigzag or blind-hem machine stitch with matching or invisible thread.

TURNED-EDGE APPLIQUÉ

1. Trace the printed reversed templates onto template plastic. Flip the template over and mark as the right side.
2. Position the template, right side up, on the right side of fabric and lightly trace, spacing images ½" apart. Cut apart, leaving a ¼" margin around the traced lines.
3. Clip curves and press edges ¼" to the wrong side around the appliqué shape.
4. Referring to the appliqué motif, pin or baste appliqué shapes to the background.
5. Hand-stitch shapes in place using a blind stitch and thread to match or machine-stitch using a short blind hemstitch and either matching or invisible thread.

Borders

Most patterns give an exact size to cut borders. You may check those sizes by comparing them to the horizontal and vertical center measurements of your quilt top.

STRAIGHT BORDERS

1. Mark the centers of the side borders and quilt top sides.
2. Stitch borders to quilt top sides with right sides together and matching raw edges and center marks using a ¼" seam. Press seams toward borders.
3. Repeat with top and bottom border lengths.

MITERED BORDERS

1. Add at least twice the border width to the border lengths instructed to cut.
2. Center and sew the side borders to the quilt, beginning and ending stitching ¼" from the quilt corner and backstitching (Figure 1). Repeat with the top and bottom borders.

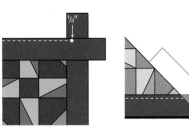

Figure 1   **Figure 2**

3. Fold and pin quilt right sides together at a 45-degree angle on one corner (Figure 2). Place a straightedge along the fold and lightly mark a line across the border ends.

4. Stitch along the line, backstitching to secure. Trim seam to ¼" and press open (Figure 3).

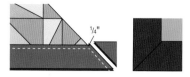

Figure 3

Quilt Backing & Batting

We suggest that you cut your backing and batting 8" larger than the finished quilt-top size. If preparing the backing from standard-width fabrics, remove the selvages and sew two or three lengths together; press seams open. If using 108"-wide fabric, trim to size on the straight grain of the fabric.

Prepare batting the same size as your backing. You can purchase prepackaged sizes or battings by the yard and trim to size.

Quilting

1. Press quilt top on both sides and trim all loose threads.
2. Make a quilt sandwich by layering the backing right side down, batting and quilt top centered right side up on flat surface and smooth out. Pin or baste layers together to hold.
3. Mark quilting design on quilt top and quilt as desired by hand or machine.
Note: If you are sending your quilt to a professional quilter, contact them for specifics about preparing your quilt for quilting.
4. When quilting is complete, remove pins or basting. Trim batting and backing edges even with raw edges of quilt top.

Binding the Quilt

1. Join binding strips on short ends with diagonal seams to make one long strip; trim seams to ¼" and press seams open (Figure 4).

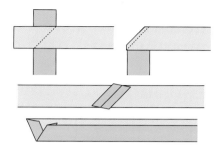

Figure 4

2. Fold 1" of one short end to wrong side and press. Fold the binding strip in half with wrong sides together along length, again referring to Figure 4; press.
3. Starting about 3" from the folded short end, sew binding to quilt top edges, matching raw edges and using a ¼" seam. Stop stitching ¼" from corner and backstitch (Figure 5).

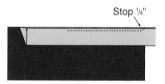

Stop ¼"

Figure 5

4. Fold binding up at a 45-degree angle to seam and then down even with quilt edges, forming a pleat at corner, referring to Figure 6.

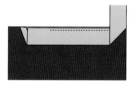

Figure 6

5. Resume stitching from corner edge as shown in Figure 6, down quilt side, backstitching ¼" from next corner. Repeat, mitering all corners, stitching to within 3" of starting point.
6. Trim binding end long enough to tuck inside starting end and complete stitching (Figure 7).

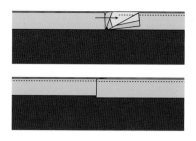

Figure 7

7. Fold binding to quilt back and stitch in place by hand or machine to complete your quilt.

QUILTING TERMS

- **Appliqué:** Adding fabric motifs to a foundation fabric by hand or machine (see Appliqué section of Basic Techniques).
- **Basting:** This temporarily secures layers of quilting materials together with safety pins, thread or a spray adhesive in preparation for quilting the layers.

  Use a long, straight stitch to hand- or machine-stitch one element to another holding the elements in place during construction and usually removed after construction.
- **Batting:** An insulating material made in a variety of fiber contents that is used between the quilt top and back to provide extra warmth and loft.
- **Binding:** A finishing strip of fabric sewn to the outer raw edges of a quilt to cover them.

  Straight-grain binding strips, cut on the crosswise straight grain of the fabric (see Straight & Bias Grain Lines illustration on the next page), are commonly used.

  Bias binding strips are cut at a 45-degree angle to the straight grain of the fabric. They are used when binding is being added to curved edges.
- **Block:** The basic quilting unit that is repeated to complete the quilt's design composition. Blocks can be pieced, appliquéd or solid and are usually square or rectangular in shape.
- **Border:** The frame of a quilt's central design used to visually complete the design and give the eye a place to rest.

- **Fabric Grain:** The fibers that run either parallel (lengthwise grain) or perpendicular (crosswise grain) to the fabric selvage are straight grain.

  Bias is any diagonal line between the lengthwise or crosswise grain. At these angles the fabric is less stable and stretches easily. The true bias of a woven fabric is a 45-degree angle between the lengthwise and crosswise grain lines.

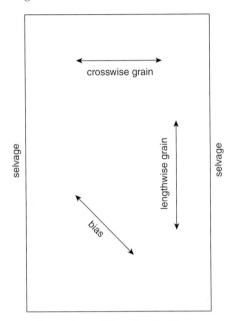

Straight & Bias Grain Lines

- **Mitered Corners:** Matching borders or turning bindings at a 45-degree angle at corners.
- **Patchwork:** A general term for the completed blocks or quilts that are made from smaller shapes sewn together.
- **Pattern:** This may refer to the design of a fabric or to the written instructions for a particular quilt design.
- **Piecing:** The act of sewing smaller pieces and/or units of a block or quilt together.

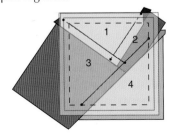

Foundation Piecing

Paper or foundation piecing is sewing fabric to a paper or cloth foundation in a certain order.

String or chain piecing is sewing pieces together in a continuous string without clipping threads between sections.

String or Chain Piecing

Pressing: Pressing is the process of placing the iron on the fabric, lifting it off the fabric and placing it down in another location to flatten seams or crease fabric without sliding the iron across the fabric.

Quilters do not usually use steam when pressing, since it can easily distort fabric shapes.

Generally, seam allowances are pressed toward the darker fabric in quilting so that they do not show through the lighter fabric.

Seams are pressed in opposite directions where seams are being joined to allow seams to butt against each other and to distribute bulk.

Seams are pressed open when multiple seams come together in one place.

If you have a question about pressing direction, consult a comprehensive quilting guide for guidance.

- **Quilt (noun):** A sandwich of two layers of fabric with a third insulating material between them that is then stitched together with the edges covered or bound.
- **Quilt (verb):** Stitching several layers of fabric materials together with a decorative design. Stippling, crosshatch, channel, in-the-ditch, free-motion, allover and meandering are all terms for quilting designs.

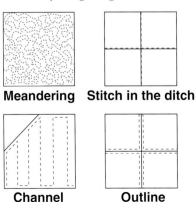

Meandering   **Stitch in the ditch**

Channel   **Outline**

- **Quilt Sandwich:** A layer of insulating material between a quilt's top and back fabric.
- **Rotary Cutting:** Using a rotary cutting blade and straightedge to cut fabric.
- **Sashing:** Strips of fabric sewn between blocks to separate or set off the designs.
- **Subcut:** A second cutting of rotary-cut strips that makes the basic shapes used in block and quilt construction.
- **Template:** A pattern made from a sturdy material which is then used to cut shapes for patchwork and appliqué quilting.

QUILTING SKILL LEVELS

- **Beginner:** A quilter who has been introduced to the basics of cutting, piecing and assembling a quilt top and is working to master these skills. Someone who has the knowledge of how to sandwich, quilt and bind a quilt, but may not have necessarily accomplished the task yet.
- **Confident Beginner:** A quilter who has pieced and assembled several quilt tops and is comfortable with the process, and is now ready to move on to more challenging techniques and projects using at least two different techniques.
- **Intermediate:** A quilter who is comfortable with most quilting techniques and has a good understanding for design, color and the whole process. A quilter who is experienced in paper piecing, bias piecing and projects involving multiple techniques. Someone who is confident in making fabric selections other than those listed in the pattern.
- **Advanced:** A quilter who is looking for a challenging design. Someone who knows she or he can make any type of quilt. Someone who has the skills to read, comprehend and complete a pattern, and is willing to take on any technique. A quilter who is comfortable in her or his skills and has the ability to select fabric suited to the project. ●